A Panorama of 5000 Years:
Korean History

A Panorama

Korean History

of 5000 Years:

By Andrew C. Nahm, Ph. D.

HOLLYM INTERNATIONAL CORP.
Elizabeth, New Jersey   Seoul

Title page: Folding screens depicting abstractly the sun and moon (king and queen), mountains, waterfalls and waves together with red pine trees and green needle clusters, symbolized the Korean people's love for the natural universe and the Yi-dynasty's royal house. This colorful assemblage can still be seen behind the royal throne chairs at both Kyŏngbok and Ch'angdŏk palaces.

Copyright © 1983
by Hollym Corporation: Publishers

All rights reserved

First published in 1983
by Hollym International Corp.
18 Donald Place,
Elizabeth, New Jersey 07208 U.S.A.

Published simultaneously in Korea
by Hollym Corporation: Publishers
14–5 Kwanchŏl-dong, Chongno-ku,
Seoul, Korea. Phone: 725-7554

ISBN: 0-930878-23-x

Library of Congress Catalog Card Number: 81-84202

한림출판사 발행
서울·종로구 관철동 14-5 전화 725-7554

Printed in Korea

To
Elizabeth and Frederick
and
Young People Like Them

PREFACE

It is difficult to compress more than 4300 years of the history into this limited amount of space and do justice to the efforts made by the Koreans who created a unique culture and established a strong national heritage. I have long felt that there was a need for a short history of Korea that dealt with both the traditional and modern periods. There has been a dire shortage of English language materials on Korean history even though there has been an increasing need in the United States for knowledge about Korea, her history and her culture.

My objective has been to present a general survey of Korean history for the benefit of the non-specialist—the general reader and young students. In this book I have endeavored to present selected historical highlights which formed the character and tradition of Korea and her people during the long period of Korean development.

There are many aspects in the history of Korea of which the Koreans are proud and worthy of praise, but there are also many shameful and unhappy events in her history. Often, Korea had been a battle ground of foreign invaders and the Korean people suffered immeasurable hardships, at one point in history even losing her sovereignty and national independence to an aggressive power. Be that as it may, the Koreans of the past ages were able to preserve their fatherland, cultivate a high cultural tradition, and protect their racial purity. In addition, by skillfully amalgamating their own ancient culture with those which were absorbed from abroad, they produced a brilliant and regenerative ethnic culture which is uniquely Korean.

The study of Korean history reveals that the Koreans were tenacious and resilient people. Undaunted, the Koreans have proven time and again that they were capable of enduring various calamities and restoring social order and economic life in times of national crisis. They amply demonstrated their ability to preserve their heritage and fatherland during times of foreign aggression, and reconstruct their national foundation afterward. Throughout the ages, the Koreans kept faith in themselves, maintaining their respect-

ability, and demonstrating their indomitable spirit.

The Romanization of Korean words, except widely known place and personal names, is in accordance with the McCune-Reischauer system. The reader will have some difficulties in pronouncing certain Korean words. The following rule will make it easier to pronounce more accurately Korean words transliterated into English.

The vowels are pronounced as follows:

a like the *a* in *father*   *e* like the *e* in *egg*
i like the *i* in *Indiana*   *o* like the *o* in *Ohio*
u like the *u* in *truth*   *o* like the *o* in *won*
ŭ like the *e* in *made*

Two vowels in a row should be pronounced separately with a few exceptions. Thus, *ai* should be read *a i* . However, *ae* is like *a* in *apple*.

Pronounce consonants as follows:

ch like *j*   *k* like *g* in *great*
p like *v*   *t* like *d* in *drive*
ch' like the *ch* in *chance* *k'* like the *k* in *king*
p' like the *p* in *pay*   *t'* like the *t* in *tank*
chch like the *j* in *Jack*   *kk* like the *g* in *god*
pp like the *b* in *bat*   *ss* like the *s* in *Sam*
tt like the *d* in *dam*

An apostrophy mark in a word, except after the consonants mentioned above, is an indication for a division of the word. For example, *Tan'gun* should be read like *tan gun,* not *tang un.*

I wish to express my sincere appreciation to my wife, Monica, who has served as a helpful critic and counselor, in addition to providing me with invaluable editorial assistance.

Kalamazoo, Michigan   A.C.N.

CONTENTS

INTRODUCTION: THE BEAUTIFUL LAND OF KOREA

Korea, with her 4300-year-old history, is one of the few oldest countries in the world. The 630 miles (1000 km) long and 120–160 miles wide Korean peninsula is situated at the eastern end of the Asiatic continent. In the north, Korea borders with Manchuria of China and the Maritime Province of the Soviet Union, and her eastern, western, and southern shores are washed by the surrounding seas. To the west of Korea across the Yellow Sea (Koreans call it the Western Sea) lies China, and to her south lie the Japanese islands, as if surrounding Korea like a fence in the sea. Thus Korea is located in the center of the East Asian world.

Present-day Korea's territory is comprised of the area below the Yalu and the Tumen rivers, but in ancient times and up to the early 10th century her vast territory included the area east of the Liao River in Manchuria and a portion of the Maritime Province of the Soviet Union. Although Korea suffers the misfortunes of being divided into north and south today, the Koreans demonstrate that they are a people with an outstanding tradition in spite of the division.

Korea, known in the West as "The Land of Morning Calm," is a beautiful country. She has four distinctive seasons. Spring is warm and long, summer is hot and humid, autumn is cool, and winter is cold. The average winter temperatures are little below 26 °F (–3 °C) in the south and 13 °F (–11 °C) in the north. Spring and autumn are breath-takingly beautiful, summer monsoons bring heavy rainfall and winter monsoons bring cold air masses from Siberia with snowfall.

Although Korea (85,360 sq. miles or 221,925 sq. km.) is only half the size of California, or one-fortieth the size of the United States, the population of South Korea today is more than 38 million and the combined population of the north and the south is over 50 million. Only about twenty per cent of her land is arable, but with her mild climate, rich soil, and industrious population, together with her abundant fishing grounds along 173,000 km. of coastlines and some 3,000 off-shore islands, Korea has all the potential of being a strong and prosperous nation.

Mt. Sŏrak in colorful autumn costume.

1 *EARLY KOREA*

IN THE BEGINNING

The Roots of the Koreans

It is not clear when the ancestors of the Koreans began to inhabit the land. Various tools of the Paleolithic Age uncovered in all parts of Korea indicated that human beings had inhabited the Korean peninsula some fifty thousand years ago. It is not clear, however, whether the people of the Paleolithic Age were the ancestors of the Koreans or not, but it is clear that people of the Neolithic Age migrated into the Korean peninsula around 4000 B. C. and left many relics behind were the ancestors.

It seems that the Neolithic people were divided into two groups. One group had inhabited the region of Mt. Paektu, spread throughout Manchuria and in the northern regions of the Korean peninsula first, and then moved southward along the west coast of Korea, occupying the central and southern regions of the peninsula. The other group came across the Tumen River from eastern Manchuria and moved southward along the east coast into the Korean peninsula. The ancient Koreans of the Yellow race, who thus created a history and nurtured a culture, were Tungusic people, cousins of the Mongols.

The "Heavenly Lake" at the summit of Mt. Paektu, the spiritual home of the Korean people.

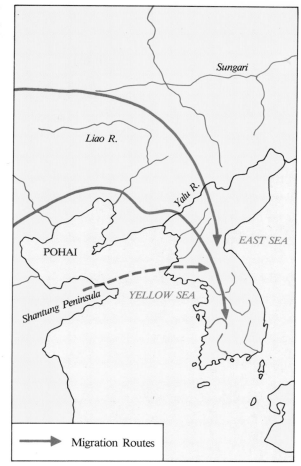

Migration Routes of Ancient Koreans.

Prehistoric Culture

Around 3000 B. C. when four great civilizations of Egypt, India, Mesopotamia, and China emerged, the ancient Koreans passed through the Neolithic culture stage, the Bronze culture stage from 1000 B. C., and then the Iron culture stage from 5th–4th century B. C. As they passed through these cultural stages, they developed a fine and unique metal culture as the ancient Korean kingdom of Chosŏn and other ancient dynasties emerged.

The agriculture that began toward the end of the Neolithic Age developed further during the Bronze Age as rice, millet, maize and other crops were cultivated and cows, horses

Stone knives. Relics of the Paleolithic Age unearthed at Sŏkchang-ri, Kongju.

13

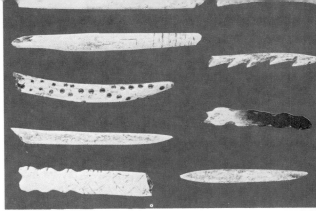

Bone tools. Fishing hooks and picks unearthed with stone and earthenwares from shell mounds.

Earthenware with straight or curved comb markings. Unearthed from a house site of the Neolithic Age at Amsa-dong, Kangdong-ku, Seoul.

and other animals were domesticated.

THE BIRTH OF THE KINGDOM OF ANCIENT CHOSŎN

There is a Tan'gun legend in connection with the founding of Ancient Chosŏn. According to a myth, Hwanung, a descendant of a celestial being who had wished to come down to the human world and establish a nation, descended upon the top of Mt. Paektu with some 3000 subordinates and founded a divine city, ruling the world and teaching the people. One day, a tiger and a bear in the mountain came to Hwanung and begged him to make them human beings. In response to their wishes, Hwanung gave them a bundle of mugwort and twenty pieces of garlic, told them to eat these and avoid the sunlight for one hundred days, after which they would become human beings. The bear, which followed the instructions of Hwanung patiently became a woman in 37 days, but the tiger could not endure and failed to become a human being. Hwanung pitied the bear which was transformed into a woman, therefore, he married her because she could not find a mate. Thus they had a son named Tan'gun who became the ancestor of the Korean people. Tan'gun united the scattered Tungusic tribes into a nation known as the Kingdom of Ancient Chosŏn and established his capital at Asadal (now P'yŏngyang) in 2333 B.C.

Painted-design pottery jar with round base, Bronze Age.

14

The dolmen discovered at Pugŭn-ri, Kanghwa Island. This type of tomb of Bronze Age has been discovered at many sites in Korea.

Although the Tan'gun legend is only a myth, it not only contains many significant historical facts, but it reflects the ideals of the Koreans as it helped them to develop a pride of being the people of a long history and ancient culture. Because of this, the Koreans preserved the legend which became the source of spiritual reawakening and solace in times of racial and national crisis.

The Struggle with the Chinese and the Fall of Ancient Chosŏn

At the end of the 3rd century B. C., China was unified into a powerful empire, with an expansionistic policy. Chosŏn fought the aggressors of China with all its strength, but it collapsed in 108 B. C. As a result, the territory of Ancient Chosŏn came under the domination of the Chinese empire of the Han dynasty, which established three commandaries (colonies) in northern Korea and a colony in the Liaotung region of Manchuria.

Meanwhile, the states of Okchŏ and Tongye emerged in the northeastern and east-central regions of the Korean peninsula. There were three tribal federations of Mahan, Chinhan, and Pyŏnhan toward the end of the 2nd century B. C. Mahan controlled the central and southern region of the peninsula, Chinhan was located in the southeast, and Pyŏnhan was in the south-central part along the south coast.

Map of three tribal states.

Iron relics. Farm implements made of iron(along with iron weapons and coins from China) were unearthed at Wiwŏn, North P'yŏngan province.

15

THE FORMATION AND DEVELOPMENT OF THE THREE KINGDOMS

From the time when the ancient Roman Empire was growing under Julius Caesar in the 1st century B. C. to the time when Christianity was spreading in the 1st century A. D., Mahan was engaged in a struggle against the Chinese and the tribes of the north, while Chinhan and Pyŏnhan contended with Japanese invaders from the south. Meanwhile, a power struggle among the three federations also grew as they were making progress in nation-building. As a result, Mahan became consolidated into the Kingdom of Paekche and Chinhan became the Kingdom of Silla. It was at this juncture that the Kingdom of Koguryŏ emerged in 37 B. C. in the southern part of Manchuria and extended its power into Korea across the Yalu River.

Each newly formed kingdom strived to promote its political and military strength with the production of iron weapons and the development of agriculture and manufacturing.

The Growth of Koguryŏ

Koguryŏ was the first one to solidify its foundation for nationhood with its center of power at Kungnaesŏng in the middle of the Yalu River region. It expanded its western frontiers as it struggled against the Chinese empire of the Han dynasty in the 3rd century, and in 313 it removed Chinese domination from Korea completely when it overthrew the Lolang commandery of the Chinese. During the reign of King Kwanggaet'o of the 5th century, the territory of Koguryŏ included the entire southern part of Manchuria and the

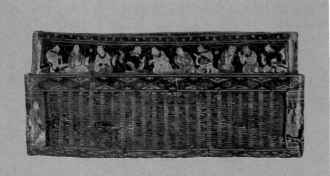

Top: Bronze mirror.
Middle: Incense burner.
Bottom: Colored design on lacquer ware.
Relics of the Lolang culture emerged in the northwestern Korea during the period of Chinese domination.

Territories of the Three Kingdoms.

Stone tablet dedicated to King Kwanggaet'o. Erected in 414 at T'ung-gu, Manchuria, it has inscriptions regarding the life and works of Kwanggaet'o. It is the largest stone tablet found to date.

northern half of the Korean peninsula.

Kwanggaet'o's son, King Changsu, moved the capital to present-day P'yŏngyang and, with ever increasing strength, he took away the northern regions of Paekche and overthrew the states of Okchŏ and Tongye, establishing the Koguryŏ domination in the area north of the Han River. Meanwhile, at the end of the 6th century, he annexed the Kingdom of Puyŏ which had existed in the north-western region of Manchuria.

The Growth and Decline of Paekche

Paekche, an aggressive tribal unit of Mahan, which was located in the fertile lower region of the Han River, gradually unified small tribal units of Mahan into a nation. During the reign of King Kŭnch'ogo of the 4th century the power of Paekche reached its zenith as it supplanted Mahan. The territory of the Kingdom of Paekche included the present Hwanghae, Kyŏnggi, North and South Ch'ungch'ŏng and Chŏlla provinces.

Facing the threats from Koguryŏ, Paekche formed an alliance with Silla, but it lost its territory along the Han River in the 5th century and moved its capital to Ungjin (now Kongju) first, and then to Sabi (now Puyŏ) in 538. King Munyŏng attempted to check the expansion of Koguryŏ, but he failed to do so.

Kaya States and the Rise of Silla

The six small tribal units of Pyŏnhan became the Kaya states. Somehow, Kaya states failed to form a unified nation, although they formed a federation for self-defense under the Kŭmgwan Kaya. Disunited, Kaya states were

17

A stone tablet commemorating the hunting expedition of King Chinhŭng.

unable to check the expansion of Silla or invasion of the Japanese, and they were taken over one by one by Silla.

Silla's evolution into a true kingdom came later than that of Koguryŏ or Paekche. However, during the reign of King Naemul of the 4th century, the power of Silla grew, and in the 5th century, a strong kingdom of Silla emerged.

Silla allied with Paekche, and it not only checked the southward expansion of Koguryŏ, but also took over the fertile Han River region from Koguryŏ during the reign of King Chinhŭng of the late 6th century. Meanwhile, Silla destroyed Kaya states in the Naktong River region and expanded its territory further to the west. With the annexation of the Kaya states, Silla grew into a strong kingdom whose territory included the fertile Kimhae and Ko-

ryŏng region, as well as the fertile region of Kyŏngju, the captial of Silla.

By the time the great migration of the Germanic people of the 4–6th centuries in Europe ended, the three unified nation-states emerged in Korea. When Silla betrayed Paekche, the Paekche-Koguryŏ alliance was formed against Silla, and a long period of warfare ensued.

KOGURYŎ'S WARS AGAINST SUI AND T'ANG CHINA

China, which had been split into many states since the early 3rd century, was reunified by the Sui dynasty at the end of the 6th century. Soon after that, Sui China mobilized a large number of troops and launched war against Koguryŏ. However, the people of Koguryŏ were united and they were able to repel the Chinese aggressors. In 612, Sui troops invaded Korea again, but Koguryŏ forces fought bravely and destroyed Sui troops everywhere. General Ŭlchi Mundŏk of Koguryŏ completely wiped out some 300,000 Sui troops which came across the Yalu River in the battles near the Salsu River (now Ch'ŏngch'ŏn River) with his ingenious military tactics. Only 2,700 Sui troops were able to flee from Korea. The Sui dynasty, which wasted so much energy and manpower in aggressive wars against Koguryŏ, fell in 618.

The T'ang dynasty of China, which overthrew the Sui dynasty and inherited its aggressive policy, launched attacks from 645 against Koguryŏ in order to re-establish Chinese domination in Korea. But Koguryŏ troops fought well, and T'ang troops invaded Korea in 645 were badly destroyed in the 60-day battles at Ansi. The victory of Koguryŏ over China was not only an example of the united effort of the people of Koguryŏ against foreign aggressors, but also a memorable event which has a significant historical meaning for the Korean people.

18

Battle scene of the Koguryŏ-T'ang war (National documentary painting).

SOCIETY AND CULTURE OF THE THREE KINGDOMS

Political and Social Systems

With the establishment of monarchal rule, the three kingdoms in Korea developed into nation-states with central bureaucracies. Government and politics were dominated by the aristocracy with the monarchy in the center, the commoners and slaves were engaged in productive works.

Silla introduced the *hwarangdo* (The Way of *Hwarang*), to train capable military leaders. Under a strict code of conduct and a highly disciplinary training, Silla produced well trained young sons of the aristocratic families known as *hwarang* (Flowery Princes), reaching the zenith of its power in the 7th century. The young aristocrats fostered their love of the land during peace time with their visits of beautiful spots in the kingdom, trained their mind and body, improved their military skills, and learned various social codes; and during times of war they fought for the country as military leaders.

Only those young aristocrats of high virtue, personal integrity and other qualities could be *hwarang.*

Thus, young *hwarang,* who were loyal leaders for the king, filial to parents, had a comradeship in trust among them, brave in battles, and prudent and respect for life, became the source of national power and contributed much to national development.

As time passed by, the form of government in each kingdom became Confucianized, and with the addition of more offices and branches of the government patterned after that of China, the power of the centralized government grew.

Gilt-bronze Maitreya of the Three Kingdom era.

Gilt-bronze Maitreya of the Three Kingdom era.

The Arrival of Buddhism

Buddhism was first introduced to Koguryŏ from China in 372. Shortly after that, in 384 an Indian monk from South China introduced Buddhism to Paekche. Meanwhile, Buddhism was introduced to Silla by a Koguryŏ monk in 527, and it spread rapidly, clashing with the deeply rooted native religious beliefs. However, Silla officially adopted Buddhism at the beginning of the 6th century, thanks to the martyrdom of a man named Yi Ch'a-don. Buddhism became not only the religion of the masses, but kings and aristocrats of Silla and Paekche also became ardent Buddhists.

The spiritual culture which they had promoted became synthesized with, and systematized under the influence of Buddhism which they embraced, and with this their culture reached a higher level. Buddhism eventually became the spiritual foundation of the nation, particularly in Paekche and Silla. As Buddhism grew, many temples and pagodas were built, many elegant statues of Buddha were produced and Buddhist arts flourished.

With the rise of Buddhism, Korea's contacts with the outside world grew, and scholarship, arts, science and technology which were imported to Korea from China, India and regions beyond brought about the enrichment of Korean culture. As a result, one of the oldest astronomical charts in the world was produced, the oldest astronomical observatory called Ch'ŏmsŏngdae was built, tumulis architecture represented by the Ssangyŏng tomb developed, and the system of doctor of medicine was established in Korea. During the Three Kingdom period, Korea's cultural progress in the fields of astronomy, mathematics, medicine, architecture and metallurgy reached the level of other advanced civilization of the world.

Ch'ŏmsŏngdae, astronomical observation tower.

Genre painting of Koguryŏ. The mural paintings of the Ssangyŏng Tomb located at Kangsŏ, South P'yŏngan province show manners and costumes of men, women and men on horseback.

The Development of Confucianism and Historical Studies

Confucianism was introduced into Korea sometime in the 1st century and greatly influenced the patterns of political and social orders in Korea. All three kingdoms realized the importance of Confucianism in regard to social morality. Koguryŏ had already established a national school in its capital at the end of the 4th century and taught Confucianism, and in Paekche and Silla the practice of Confucian morality was encouraged. The Code of *hwarang* included Confucian moral codes.

With the introduction of the Confucian classics and Chinese Buddhist texts, the knowledge of the Chinese language grew and the use of Chinese characters spread. The growth of Confucian studies and writing in Chinese brought about the development of historical

Tile with landscape in relief of the Paekche period.

Hunting scene of Koguryŏ warriors. The mural paintings on the eastern wall of the Muyong Tomb located in T'ung-gu, Manchuria.

knowledge and a literary culture in Korea.

A Korean writing system known as *idu* was developed in which the Koreans used Chinese characters to transcribe Korean words in writing. A scholar named Sŏl Ch'ong of Silla systematized and refined the *idu* system. Many books were now written by Korean scholars as a literary culture developed. Each kingdom produced its own national history in writing in order to boast its cultural superiority at home and abroad.

The Artistry of the Koreans

Chinese sources referred to the Koreans as "the people who loved singing and dancing." Indeed, the Koreans loved to sing and dance from early times. Most of their songs and dances were associated with religious rituals, but gradually more and more secular songs appeared during the Three Kingdom period, particularly in Silla.

As the number of songs increased, many musical instruments were created. Wang San-ak of Koguryŏ who wrote some 100 songs made improvements on a Chinese musical instrument and produced a six-stringed zither known as the *kŏmungo*. Paekkyŏl of Silla became famous with the writing of a song known as *panga t'aryŏng,* which is still sung. A 12-stringed zither known as the *kayagŭm* was created by the people of Kaya.

Outstanding and skillful artists of the Three Kingdom period produced numerous masterpieces in architecture, sculpture, handicrafts, and painting in association with Buddhism.

The outstanding artistic skills of Koguryŏ can be seen in the mural paintings on the interior walls of the royal tombs of Ssangyŏng and Muyong in T'unggu, former capital of Koguryŏ, and tombs uncovered in the Kangsŏ region in South P'yŏngan province.

Several tombs of the kings of Paekche near Kongju and Puyŏ were discovered, and the interior design and artifacts found in the tomb of King Munyŏng of Paekche, which was discovered recently, testify to the remarkable artistic qualities and architectural skills of Paekche workers.

Tombs of Silla kings which have been excavated had no mural paintings, but the painting of a flying horse on a saddle discovered from a royal tomb (Ch'ŏnmach'ong, or the Tomb of the Flying Horse) located in Kyŏngju, former capital of Silla, amply dem-

Interior of the tomb of King Munyŏng. The tomb located at near Kongju was discovered in 1971. Its brick walls and stone structure of the tomb show high quality interior design and engineering technology of the period.

The Flying Horse. The famous painting of flying horse on a saddle, surrounded by floral design, Silla period.

Roof tiles with surface design in Paekche period.

A stone pagoda. This is located on the ground where the Mirŭk (Maitreya) temple once stood.

A Five-story stone pagoda. It is located on the ground where the Chŏngnim temple once stood, and is one of the two stone pagodas of Paekche which exist today.

onstrates outstanding the artistic talent of Silla painters.

Solgŏ of Silla, who painted an old pine tree on the wall of the Hwangyong temple, was one of the most outstanding painters of the Three Kingdom period. It is said that his painting of an old pine tree was so realistic that many birds tried to fly into it.

There were numerous royal tombs of Silla rulers in and around Kyŏngju, but only a few were excavated. Objects such as crowns, belts, bracelets, buckles, rings, and earrings made of gold, and other decorative articles which were found in the Kŭmgwan, Sŏbong, and Ch'ŏnma tombs are outstanding specimens of artistic works of superior quality of the Silla people.

Almost all sculpture and stone reliefs of the period were inspired by Buddhism. Many Buddha statues were produced in gold, silver, iron, copper and granite. Even roof tiles with exquisite designs and bricks of the period amply witness skills and taste of workmen of the Three Kingdom period.

A Golden Crown of Silla. A golden crown made in the 5-6th century has the shape of a Chinese character 出 and many small jade stones on its branches.

Stone pagoda of the Punhwang temple near Kyŏngju. The only surviving stone pagoda of the pre-unified Silla period. Only three lower stories are remaining today.

Introduction of Culture of the Three Kingdoms to Japan

While engaged in a power struggle among themselves, the three kingdoms actively promoted intercultural exchange. At the same time, they established cultural relations with China and helped the Japanese to lay their cultural foundation by exporting Confucianism and Buddhism to Japan.

The contribution made by Paekche to the development of a new culture in Japan was enormous. In the 6th century Paekche sent Confucian scholars such as Achikki and Wang In who enlightened the Japanese with Confucianism and Buddhism and introduced book learning. More scholars, monks, and skilled workers were dispatched to Japan in the following century, and Confucian doctors, Buddhist monks, medical doctors, historians and artists and technicians of Paekche who went to Japan

The best known gilt bronze statue of the Bodhisattva Kwanŭm produced in Paekche. Unearthed in Puyŏ, seeing from front and side.

A pair of gold pendants. Hollow globular objects decorate the link, on which a three-leaf ornament is hanging.

left behind many historic and cultural monuments in the Nara region of Japan. Koguryŏ monks also went to Japan and became leaders of the Buddhist world of Japan. Monk Hyeja of Koguryŏ was Prince Shōtoku's teacher, and a Korean monk and painter named Tamjing taught the Japanese a new religion as well as a new art. The famous mural painting of the Hōryū temple near Nara is the copy of Tamjing's painting. A tree named *Kudaragi*(Paekche tree in Japanese) which the Koreans planted is still standing in the grounds of Hōryū temple.

The Koreans who went to Japan also taught the Japanese art of painting, music, philosophy, and agricultural skills as well as religion. The rise of the Asuka culture and the emergence of a unified nation-state in Japan had much to do with the culture which the Japanese had imported from Korea.

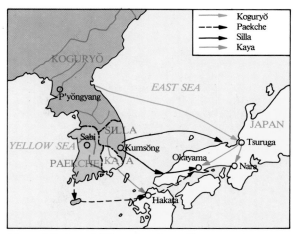

Map of Cultural Migration from Korea to Japan.

The Cliff of *Nakhwa*(Falling Flowers). It is said that some 3,000 court ladies of Paekche jumped from the cliff into the waters of the Kŭm River when foreign troops invaded the capital.

The Art Museum of Puyŏ where artistic accomplishments of the Paekche people are housed.

THE EMERGENCE OF UNIFIED KOREA AND INTERNAL DEVELOPMENT

The Unification of the Three Kingdoms

In the middle of the 6th century when Europe witnessed the rise of the Frankish kingdom and the transition to medieval society, Silla took over the Han River region. At this juncture, Koguryŏ and Paekche formed an alliance against Silla. Meanwhile, Japan became an ally of Paekche. Faced with this situation, Silla allied with T'ang China. The combined forces of Silla and T'ang China were too powerful for Paekche; She fell in 660. Soon after the overthrow of Paekche, Silla and Chinese forces turned against Koguryŏ, and Koguryŏ fell in 668.

The Silla-T'ang China alliance was soon broken when the Chinese refused to leave Korea after the destruction of Koguryŏ. Silla won the support of the people in former territories of Paekche and Koguryŏ and fought successful battles against Chinese troops, forcing them to withdraw. With this, Silla brought about the unification of Korea.

The fact that Silla was able to preserve her national independence and establish the territorial unity of the Korean people following her victory over Chinese troops has great historical significance. Only because Silla was able to establish territorial unity in Korea was it possible for the Koreans to maintain unity and an autonomous historical development and bring about a greater social and cultural progress.

Politics and Society of Unified Korea

Silla, reorganized many systems of the kingdom in order to administer the expanded territory and govern the people better. In conjunction with structural reforms, Silla imported T'ang systems and culture, carefully blending them with traditional systems and culture

The tomb of General Kim Yu-sin of Silla who contributed to the unification of Korea.

P'osŏk pavilion grounds. Foundation stones of the P'osŏk pavilion which was located in Kyŏngju show a glimpse of the extravagant life that aristocrats enjoyed.

in an endeavor to bring about a new civilization. As a result, during the 8th century, the firm foundation of the nation of homogeneous people was constructed and national culture grew.

Silla also sought to establish peaceful relations with her neighbors. She sent envoys to T'ang China and established cordial relations with China. Many students and monks who were sent to China received advanced education there. Some Koreans who passed Chinese civil service examination worked for the government of T'ang China. Others returned to Silla after receiving a higher education and brought T'ang culture to Korea, contributing much to economic, cultural and social progress in Silla. A balance of power that developed between Silla, Parhae, T'ang China and Japan in northeast Asia enabled them to maintain a peace for a considerable period of time.

The power of the monarchy was strengthened, and the bureaucracy of the central government became more efficient. New laws adopted improved the system of justice, and with the establishment of subcapitals and more local governments and military posts throughout the kingdom, law and order were improved. The government of Silla became increasingly Confucianized. A significant change in politics was the replacement of the royal house of the Pak clan by the Kim clan in the 7th century.

The social structure of unified Korea remained the same as before, with the aristocracy as the ruling class. The vast majority of the people who were commoners tilled the land as tenants, and the "low-born" people were engaged in various types of productive work, supporting the extravagant life of the aristocracy, the owners of the most of the farmlands. War prisoners became slaves, joining the ranks of others who already were. The aristocracy was exempted from tax payment, and the tax burden fell heavily on the commoners and people of low birth.

In the 8th century the capital city of Kyŏngju, where most of the aristocrats lived, grew into a large metropolis with more than 180,000 households and a population of one million. All its houses had tiled roofs. Charcoal was used to cook food, and it is recorded that there was the sound of music day and night in the city.

With agriculture as the main economic activity, handicrafts and other industries developed as the supply of food and commodities became abundant. The technology to produce silk and other cloth, golden and silver artifacts, iron, and lacquer ware advanced. Silla exported its goods, to China, Japan, and other countries.

29

THE CULTURE OF UNIFIED KOREA

Cushioned by a stable social order and assisted by a growing economy, Silla fostered a brilliant culture with the cultural heritage of the previous ages as a foundation. Silla achieved a remarkable cultural synthesis by amalgamating its own culture with those of Paekche and Koguryŏ, as well as the newly imported T'ang culture. A splendid Korean culture flourished and bloomed during the 8th and 9th centuries, bringing the Golden Age of Buddhism in Korean history.

Buddhism became deeply rooted in the fertile Korean soil as it won the adherence, not only of the kings, queens, and aristocrats, but also of the common people. Many Buddhist sects arose, a large number of beautiful Buddhist temples were constructed, and a number of outstanding scholar-monks appeared. Many magnificent Buddhist temples which were constructed during the Golden Age of Buddhism were the Pulguk, the Haein, the Pusŏk, and the Hwaŏm temples.

There were many outstanding scholar-monks and it is said that nine out of ten Silla people became Buddhists. Many Silla monks travelled to India and China. Hyech'o, one of those who visited foreign lands, wrote a valuable book on India and Indian culture.

As Confucian influence grew strong in Silla, many outstanding scholars, such as Sŏl Ch'ong and Ch'oe Ch'i-wŏn, emerged. Ch'oe Ch'i-wŏn was educated in China, passed the Chinese civil service examination, and worked for the T'ang government for a while. His literary quality was highly praised in Silla as well as in China. Under the influence of the Confucian scholars the strength of Confucianism grew and it eventually became the leading ideology of the new dynasty of Koryŏ which emerged later. Meanwhile, knowledge of mathematics, astronomy, science of divination, medicine, and military art developed

rapidly.

As religion and scholarship advanced, the printing techniques were improved to print

Buddhist texts and Confucian classics. The
Buddhist text called *Tarani,* recently discovered from the three story Sŏkka (Sakyamuni)

The Pulguk temple in Kyŏngju. It was built in 751
A.D. Stone stairways and stone structures are
original.

Right: The Tabo Pagoda of the Pulguk temple.

Opposite page: The Sŏkka (Sakyamuni) Pagoda, a stone pagoda dedicated to Sakyamuni. Twenty-seven feet high, it is regarded as the most elegant stone pagoda in Korea.

Pagoda of the Pulguk temple, is believed to have been printed before 751, the year in which the Sŏkka Pagoda was constructed, and it is regarded as the oldest Buddhist text printed with wooden blocks in the world. Silla produced 4,745 wooden printing blocks for a Buddhist text.

There was great artistic activity at this time, clearly evidenced by the various handicraft goods which were used by aristocrats as well as in pagodas, Buddhist statues, and huge bronze bells that were installed in Buddhist temples.

The finest examples of Buddhist architecture of Silla are the Pulguk temple and the Sŏkkuram grotto temple in Kyŏngju. The wooden buildings of the Pulguk temple were burned down by the Japanese who invaded Korea in 1592 and only stone structures remained. In the latter part of the Yi period (1392–1910) some buildings were rebuilt.. The present-day Pulguk temple buildings are ones which were constructed recently in their original forms. The stone arch-bridges of the Blue Cloud and the White Cloud leading to the main entrance of the Pulguk temple are two of many masterpieces of Silla architecture, and two stone pagodas of the Sŏkka (Sakyamuni) and the Tabo which stand in the main courtyard also show the high architectural taste and skills of the unified Silla period. Unlike Chinese and Japanese pagodas which were built with bricks or wood, Silla's stone pagodas have uncomparable technical superiority and harmonious beauty.

Above: 11-headed Avalokitesvara made of granite in Sŏkkuram grotto near Kyŏngju, 751 A. D.
Below: Two deva kings guarding the Buddha statue in the Sŏkkuram grotto in Kyŏngju.
Opposite page: Central Buddha statue in Sŏkkuram grotto high on a ridge in Kyŏngju. Along with bas-reliefs of other Buddhist images and guardian dieties, it is among the finest works of Buddhist art.

34

The bell of the Pongdŏk temple with bas-reliefs. Produced in 771, it is the largest bronze bell of Silla.

Pongdŏk temple bronze bell angel.

Sangwŏn temple bronze bell angels.

Kwaenŭng, the tomb of the King Wŏnsŏng, Silla period.

Many large bronze bells with beautiful bas-reliefs were produced and were installed in Buddhist temples. One of Silla bells in 11 feet (360 cm.) high and 4.5 feet (140 cm.) wide in diameter at the bottom. Most Silla bells have a mellow sound which invoked reverent feelings.

Silla's *hyangga* (native songs) of the pre-unified period developed further as many more songs were produced. Most of them had a Buddhist flavor. Some of them were prayers in nature, some were praises for the benevolent and merciful Buddha, and some were secular songs. The *hyangga,* while being an inseparable part of Silla's religious culture, also reflect the sentiments of the people of Silla.

THE FALL OF SILLA

The unity of peace of Silla, which lasted some 100 years after the unification of the three kingdoms, was broken due to the power struggle between the aristocrats which reached a climax in the 8th century.

Failing to read the signs of the time, aristocrats continued to live extravagantly, creating heavier burdens for the common people. As social chaos grew, the morale of the people declined, and the influence and prestige of the government rapidly deteriorated.

In 935 the last king of Silla surrendered to Koryŏ which rose in 918.

37

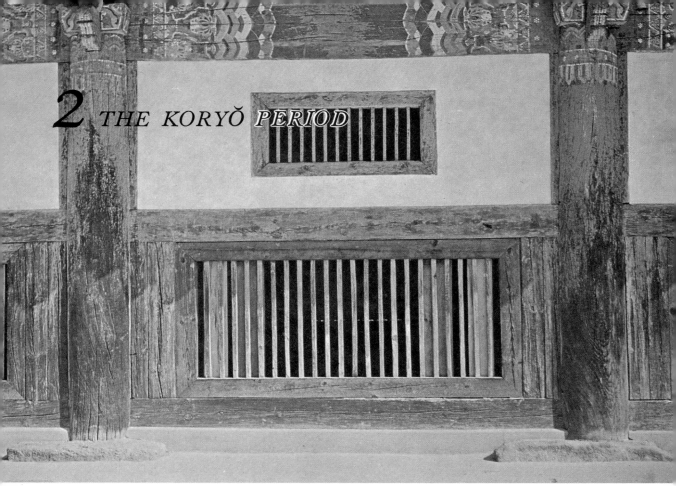

2 THE KORYŎ PERIOD

The outer wall with air ventilation system of the Haein temple. The *Tripitaka Koreana* is stored in a unique storage hall. The exposed wooden structural pieces are painted in five colors known as *tanch'ŏng*.

THE FOUNDING OF THE KINGDOM OF KORYŎ

General Wang Kŏn founded a new dynasty in 918. He named it Koryŏ, symbolizing that it was the successor to Koguryŏ. Korea (Corea) became known in the West by the name of the new kingdom. The Koryŏ period in Korean history lasted to 1392.

Wang Kŏn and his immediate successors established an efficient central bureaucracy patterned after the Chinese and divided the kingdom into provinces, prefectures, subprefectures, districts and smaller administrative units. Military bases and guard posts were established throughout the country and frontier defenses were strengthened. For the first time, the whole kingdom was governed by a salaried bureaucracy, and in 958 the Chinese civil service examination system was adopted as a means of selecting officials.

T'aejo made the promotion of unity and harmony of the people, his principal policy of nation-building. He enlisted the support of the local aristocrats, incorporated the scattered Koguryŏ people of the state of Parhae, which was overthrown in 926, and employed Silla and Paekche people in the new government. He made peace overtures to the last king of Silla and persuaded him to surrender peacefully to Koryŏ in 935.

Administrative Districts of Koryŏ.

THE DEVELOPMEMT OF AN ARISTOCRATIC SOCIAL ORDER

A closed, hereditary aristocracy emerged in Koryŏ. The officialdom of Koryŏ, which included only aristocratic families, with large kinship units, was divided into a high official class and a lower official class which included petty government functionaries.

Below the aristocracy were the common (*yangmin,* or good people) who paid taxes and provided military service. Most of the commoners were peasants who tilled the land owned by aristocrats, but the commoner class also included artisans and merchants.

Below the commoner class was the "low-born" people group which included public and private slaves, government workers in mines and porcelain kilns, butchers, some peasants, and those who were engaged in "undesirable" and unclean professions. Slaves were bought and sold. Children born of slaves automatically became slaves.

The commoners, like aristocrats, had large kinship units. Needless to say, there was no upward social mobility. A majority of the top-ranking aristocrats lived either in the capital or in the Metropolitan District. The civil officials enjoyed more prestige and had more power than the military officers.

Although the Koryŏ society was dominated by the aristocracy, it had many systems which were established for the welfare of the people. For example, "righteous granaries" were built to store grains in times of abundant

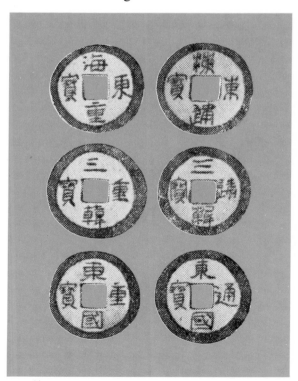

Koryŏ coins.

39

harvest in order to help the poor in times of severe food shortage through the system of grain loans.

Koryŏ's economy was agriculture as the main economic activity. Although foreign trade and exportation of Koryŏ celadon wares existed, foreign trade as a whole declined after the collapse of the firm of Chang Po-go of the Silla period. However, the growing domestic trade necessitated the coinage of money called *Haedongt'ongbo* as more Chinese coins were imported and used.

Among various seasonal festivals and folk activities were the Lantern Festival of Buddhism and the *P'algwan* Festival, which was associated with native religious practices intended to bring harmony between man and the spirits of the mountains and rivers. Among folk festivals were *Tano* (the 5th day of the 5th month of the lunar calendar) on which day the commoners enjoyed wrestling matches and swing contests, the "hair-washing" festival of the 6th month of the lunar calendar, and *Ch'usŏk,* the harvest festival (the full-moon festival) of the 15th day of the 8th month of the lunar calendar, which has been one of the major festivals since the time of the three kingdoms. The Koreans played field hockey and other games.

THE STRUGGLE AGAINST THE NORTHERN AGGRESSORS

The Khitans rose in Mongolia and established the Liao dynasty in the early 10th century, and some 800,000 Khitans invaded Korea in 994 in order to force Korea to acknowledge the suzerainty of the Liao dynasty. The Khitans raided Koryŏ repeatedly. In 1011 they even captured the capital of Koryŏ. However, the Khitans who invaded again in 1018 met disaster at the hand of Korean troops under General Kang Kam-ch'an in the great battle of Kwiju, and the entire Khitan army was destroyed.

Koryŏ keenly felt the need for a strong national defense and constructed defensive walls around the capital, as well as a long wall between the mouth of the Yalu River and Toryŏnp'o on the east coast.

Statue of Kang Kam-ch'an.

Opposite page: (Above) The Naksŏngdae. General Kang Kam-ch'an's tomb and monument. (Below) Battle scene of Koryŏ-Khitan War at Kwiju.

The National game of *Kyŏkku*. *Kyŏkku* or polo was played at a national stadium in the capital.

THE MONGOL INVASIONS AND DECLINE OF KORYŎ

The Mongol Empire which rose under Genghis Khan in the early 13th century fostered its aggressiveness toward China and Korea, posing a greater threat to Korea than the Khitan of the Jurched. In 1225, it pressured Koryŏ to sever its ties with the Chinese, and in 1231, when Koryŏ refused, the hordes of the Mongols poured into Korea. The Koryŏ dynasty moved its capital to Kanghwa Island, off Inch'ŏn of today. There were six invasions of the Mongols during the next two and an half decades during which the country suffered great devastation.

After moving the capital to Kanghwa Island, Koryŏ fought defensive wars against the Mongols and eventually peace was established between Koryŏ and the Mongols. Koryŏ was forced to acknowledge the suzerainty of the Mongol dynasty (Yuan) in China. It is said that the Mongols took away over 206,000 male captives and a large number of women from Korea during their invasion of 1254 alone.

The capital of Koryŏ returned to Kaegyŏng with the conclusion of peace with the Mongols, but the Mongols left deep scars in Korea.

The Mongols. A battle scene.

KORYŎ CULTURE

Buddhism
Buddhism grew stronger during the Koryŏ period and became the dominant force in Koryŏ culture. Under government sponsorship, it became a state religion and many beautiful Buddhist temples were built. As the number of monasteries grew, a hierarchical structure of the Buddhist church emerged. The number of converts to Buddhism increased vastly and by the 13th century, various sects took deep roots in Korea.

The Printing of Buddhist Texts
One of the most outstanding cultural accomplishments of Koryŏ was the improvement of printing skills. Silla had already produced wooden printing blocks to print Buddhist texts. Koryŏ improved printing techniques, and printed a large volume *Tripitaka* in the early 13th century with newly carved movable wooden printing blocks. However, they were destroyed by the Mongols.

During the period when the Koryŏ court was located on Kanghwa Island, a new set of 81,137 printing blocks, each measuring eight by twenty-seven inches, was carved and the *Tripitaka Koreana* was printed in 1251. These movable wooden printing blocks are now preserved in the Haein temple. Meanwhile, the Koryŏ printers produced movable metal type some 200 years before Johann Gutenberg's invention in Germany.

The Development of Confucianism and Scholarship
If Buddhism was the popular religion, Confucianism was the political ideology of the government. With the adoption of the Chinese civil examination system, all those who as-

Opposite page: Wooden printing blocks for the *Tripitaka Koreana*.

42

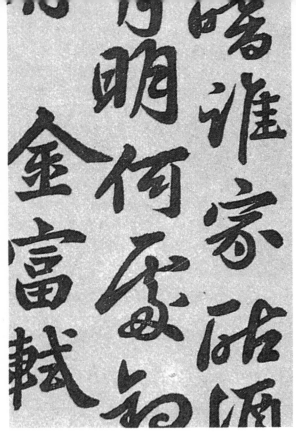

Calligraphy of Kim Pu-sik.

Original text of the *Samguk sagi*

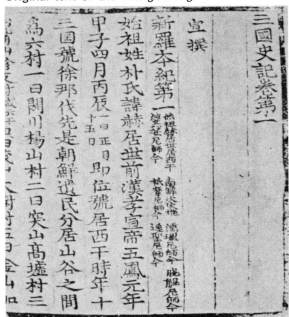

pired to become officials had to pass national civil service examinations in various categories. Studies in Confucian classics flourished, producing many outstanding scholars.

Toward the end of the Koryŏ period, Neo-Confucianism was introduced to Korea. Unlike the orthodox Confucianism which stressed textual interpretation, Neo-Confucianism emphasized philosophical and metaphysical studies on universal principles of man and his nature.

The growing influence of Confucian academicians induced the growth of historical studies. Among the most important works were the *Samguk sagi* (History of the Three Kingdoms) by Kim Pu-sik, published in 1145, and the *Samguk yusa* (Memorabilia of the Three Kingdoms) by Ilyŏn, published in 13th century. They are the chief sources of our knowledge of early Korean history. Among some of the oldest books was a massive work of 50 volumes printed in 1234, but destroyed during the

Portrait of An Hyang, who introduced Neo-Confucianism to Korea.

Mongol invasion. Another book printed in 1337 is now preserved in Paris at the National Museum of France.

The Korean traders who came in contact with the Arab traders in China brought cotton goods, gun powder, spices, drugs, and a new calendar into Korea. The introduction of new knowledge on astronomy, geography, and mathematics also enhanced the cultural development of Koryŏ. The introduction of bookkeeping systems, new agricultural methods and other technology helped the commercial and technical growth of the Koreans.

With the introduction of cotton seeds from China in the middle of the 14th century, the Koreans cultivated cotton and produced new materials. Meanwhile, the techniques of gun powder production were learned and from 1377 Koryŏ manufactured firearms. Naval vessels equipped with firearms helped to ward off attacks by Japanese pirates.

The Muryangsu Hall. One of the oldest wooden building of Korea.

Koryŏ Arts, Architecture and Crafts

In the field of architecture, Buddhism contributed much as such renowned buildings as Muryangsu Hall of the Pusŏk temple and the Main Hall of the Sudŏk temple were constructed.

Among stone structures of the Koryŏ period which still remain are six-cornered and eight-cornered pagodas and those pagodas called *pudo* which were built to bury high ranking monks. The ten-story marble pagoda of the Kyŏngch'ŏn temple is among the most beautiful pagodas of Korea.

Among the sculpture of the Koryŏ period are statues of Buddha and stone lanterns. The statue of Bodhisattva Amithabha made of clay is one of the most beautiful and representative sculptural masterpieces of Koryŏ.

Clay Seated Buddha at Pusŏk temple.

The Chinese music which Korea imported during the T'ang and the Sung periods, known as the *T'angak* or *a-ak* (elegant music) in Korea, flourished along with the traditional music of the Koreans called *hyangak*. Whereas Chinese music became the music of Confucian ceremonies and the court rituals, accompanying certain forms of dances, the *hyangak* remained the music of the people. With the introduction of Chinese music, many new musical instruments were either imported or created. Old musical instruments such as *kŏmungo* and *kayagŭm* remained popular, and the hourglass-shaped drum called *changgo* became a most widely used musical instrument in Korea. The music of Shamanism remained strong.

The Kyŏngch'ŏn Pagoda temple. This is now located in the grounds of the Kyŏngbok palace in Seoul. Height: 13m.

The World Renowned Koryŏ Celadon: Its Beauty and Secrets

The most precious cultural property of Koryŏ is its celadon. Improving upon the ceramic art of Sung China, the potters of Korea employed at government kilns produced highly praised Koryŏ celadon. The pale green Koryŏ celadon wares, with their graceful and elegant shapes and lovely surface designs executed in inlayed clays of white or grey colors, surpassed all others in beauty and quality. Some of the most superb examples were the *sanggam* green celadon wares. During the 13th century, a new form of pottery uniquely

The *sanggam* celadon of pale blue color is an example of highest artistic achievements of Koryŏ. Its artistic value is widely recognized throughout the world.

Korean developed. Unfortunately, during the Mongol invasions, the secrets of Koryŏ celadon were lost.

In addition to green celadon wares of various shapes and designs, the Korean potters produced elegant white, black and greyish celadon wares. However, the green celadon wares were superior in beauty and quality with designs of flowers, floating clouds, cranes and swallows in flight, mountains and streams, and weeping willow trees.

47

Koryŏ celadon vase.

THE FALL OF KORYŎ

The Restoration Movement of King Kongmin

King Kongmin (1351–74) carried out various reform measures to restore national strength, reduce the power of aristocrats and powerful families as well as that of the military groups, and deal with external threats. However, the debate over foreign policy created an extremely bitter political controversy. Some advocated the maintenance of an alliance with the Mongols but others advocated a pro-Ming policy. The Chinese overthrew the Yuan dynasty and established the Ming dynasty in 1368. As a result, aspiration of King Kongmin were frustrated as he met the determined opposition of his enemies. Those kings who came after him were inept.

The Invasion of the Red Turbans and Japanese Pirates

Hordes of northern nomads called Red Turbans invaded Korea twice toward the middle of the 14th century, and during the second invasion of 1361, they captured the capital of Koryŏ. Koryŏ troops under General Yi Sŏng-gye were able to repulse the invaders, but the fate of Koryŏ was already sealed.

To make matters worse, Japanese pirates rampaged along the southern and western coasts of Korea, plundering towns and villages. Koryŏ troops under Generals Ch'oe Yŏng and Yi Sŏng-gye, together with naval vessels were able to expel Japanese pirates from Korean soil, destroying some 500 Japanese pirate ships and destroyed bases. However, the military efforts of Koryŏ drained her national strength, causing severe financial difficulties to rise.

The End of the Koryŏ Dynasty

The Koryŏ court sent General Yi Sŏng-gye to the Yalu region to cooperate with the Mongols against Ming China and the Red Turbans. General Yi, however, brought his troops back

Japanese pirate.

Portrait of Chŏng Mong-ju.

to the capital and in 1388 carried out a coup against the king. After eliminating his enemies, he placed a new king on the throne and usurped the royal prerogatives, sending many of his enemies into exile. He exiled the last king of Koryŏ in 1392. It was at this juncture that a highly respected scholar named Chŏng Mong-ju, who was loyal to the Koryŏ dynasty, was assassinated. This marked the collapse of the Koryŏ dynasty which had ruled Korea for 475 years.

49

3 THE YI PERIOD: THE RISE OF A CONFUCIANIZED SOCIETY

The Administration Hall of the Kyŏngbok palace.

THE FOUNDING OF THE KINGDOM OF CHOSŎN

The Yi dynasty which Yi Sŏng-gye established in 1392 lasted until 1910. Yi Sŏng-gye became known by his posthumous title of T'aejo(Grand Progenitor) of the new dynasty. Korea was renamed Chosŏn, or the Land of Morning Calm.

A completely new capital city (Sŏul, or Seoul in Korean) was built. It was surrounded by an inner and outer defensive walls. The city inside the inner wall with massive East, South, and West gates, was divided into wards by checkerboard fashioned boulevards and streets. New government buildings, palace buildings, and ancestral shrines were con-structed.

T'aejo and his successors, particularly the 4th monarch, Sejong (1418–1450) built a strong foundation for the dynasty. They renovated the government structure, strengthened national defense, and promoted the economy and culture of the kingdom. In the early stage of the Yi period, the northern-most parts of the peninsula were pacified, and national boundaries of Korea were established along the Yalu and Tumen rivers. Korea became a tribute state to Ming China.

The kingdom was divided into eight provinces, and each province was divided into prefectures, countries, and other smaller administrative districts.

Portrait of Yi T'aejo.

SOCIETY OF CHOSŎN

Politics

Confucian political principles guided the conduct of the government and the officials. The top government officials were classified into nine ranks, and each rank had a senior and a junior member. Government officials were those who passed Confucian civil service examinations.

Social Structure

The social order and the pattern of behavior of the people were established on Confucian precepts. Accordingly, the people were classified into four classes—the *yangban* (nobility), the *chungin* (middle people), the *sangmin*

Eight provinces of Chosŏn.

or *sangin* (commoners), and the *ch'ŏnmin* (lowborn). The *yangban,* or the nobility, included high ranking civil and military officials and their families, and the civil officials were called the eastern branch as a collective body, and the military officials were called the western branch. The civil branch enjoyed superior political power. The members of the *yangban* class who received government appointments received appropriate amount of land grants as their source of income according to their ranks.

The "rank-stones." They were placed in front of the Administrative Building in the Kyŏngbok palace designating places for ministers according to their ranks.

The commoner class included those who tilled the land as tenant farmers, artisans and merchants who paid taxes and served in the military as conscripts. The lowborn class included public and private slaves, domestic servants, as well as public entertainers, Shamans and Buddhist priests, butchers, grave-diggers, female entertainers called *kisaeng,* and others who were engaged in unclear professions.

The social status of individuals was hereditary, except in some unusual cases. There was little upward social mobility. Intermarriages or social interactions between the *yangban* and the commoners and others were virtually forbidden, and rules and social conventions were strictly enforced in order to maintain the hierarchical social order based on Confucianism.

Although the clan structure and extended family system were more important to the *yangban* class, the Koreans as a whole maintained an extended family system headed by a patriarch. The clan members who had a common ancestor established an ancestral shrine in the village where the clan headquarters was located, and kept their records of genealogy. Marriages between members of the same clan, no matter how distantly related, were strictly forbidden. Filial piety was regarded as a cardinal principle, Confucian precepts and rituals were faithfully observed, and the authority of male heads of families was kept intact while the fidelity and obedience of a wife to her husband as well as children to the father was absolutely required. Those filial children and virtuous women who sacrificed themselves for their parents or husbands were honored along with officials loyal to the king.

Kŭmgwan chobok (front) Kŭmgwan chobok (back) Samo kwandae Chŏllic

Uniforms of civil and military officials.

A 3-day celebration for a successful candidate for the highest degree.

Korean traditional marriage ceremony.

Participation of women in social activities was not permitted, and the remarriage of widows was forbidden. Needless to say, the Korean society of the Yi period was a *yangban* dominated and male-oriented society. The civility of the people was equated with subservience to the *yangban* and those who occupied higher hierarchical positions.

Education and Civil Service Examination System

The most common way in which one became a government official was by passing a civil service examination, the system which was imported from China. Those who passed literary examinations on Confucian classics, history and literary arts became civil officials. The miscellaneous category included such disciplines as medicine, astronomy, mathematics, and foreign (Chinese) language. Only sons of the *yangban* families were permitted to take literary and military examinations.

In order to produce well educated candidates, the government established in 1398, the highest academic institution called the Sŏnggyun'gwan. Confucian schools were established throughout the country. Many privately

A picture of filial piety.

53

established high level schools called *sŏwŏn* were established and produced many well-educated students. Private primary schools (*sŏdang*) were established by Confucian teachers in Seoul, towns and villages.

Educational opportunities were almost entirely limited to the sons of the *yangban* and *chungin* families.

Economy and Land System

The government maintained a strong anti-

The Myŏngnyun Hall, part of Sŏnggyun'gwan, the highest Confucian academy in Seoul built in 1393.

commercialism, and discouraged the growth of commercial economy. However, as the population grew, especially in the capital, and commerce developed, the government issued licences to certain designated merchants to establish specialized shops on what is now Chongno Street in Seoul. Commercial transactions in rural Korea were carried out by peddlers and at regional markets which were

Tosan *sŏwon* built in 1552 at Andong.

Traditional primary school called *sŏdang*.

54

opened once every five days.

Agriculture was the economic foundation of the nation and it was the economic basis of the officialdom of the *yangban* class. Only a very small number of peasants had small plots of land of their own. Thus, the system of land grants given to the *yangban* people brought about a new landlordism.

Foreign trade played an insignificant part in the Korean economy. Almost all foreign trade was between Korea and China, and the limited foreign trade which had existed between Korea and Japan were suspended after 1592. More money came into circulation, but barter was a common means of commercial transactions, particularly in rural Korea.

THE DEVELOPMENT OF NATIONAL CULTURE

The Creation of Han'gŭl

Among the many outstanding cultural accomplishments was the creation of a unique Korean writing system. King Sejong, who believed that the Korean people ought to have their own writing system, collaborated with the scholars of the Academy of Scholars (Chiphyŏnjŏn) in order to create a Korean alphabet which was appropriate to Korean spoken language, easy to learn and express thoughts freely in writing. As a result, twenty-eight alphabetical letters collectively known as *han'gŭl* (Korean letters) were invented, and in 1446 King Sejong promulgated it as *Hunmin chŏngŭm,* and the Koreans became the possessors of their own writing system.

Statue of Sejong

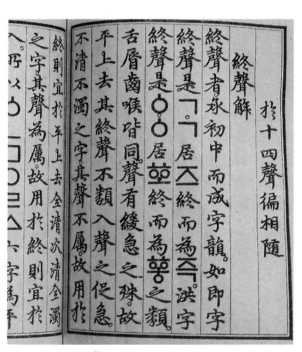

Hunmin chŏngŭm with annotations. *Han'gŭl* is a scientific and ingenious creative alphabet.

測雨臺

乾隆庚寅五月□

A metal rain guage produced in 1770.

Science and Technology

Scientists and technicians of the Yi period achieved many remarkable things, especially in printing. The movable metal type of the Koryŏ period was improved on at the government type casting shop and superior quality books were printed.

Rain gauges were created and in 1422 they were installed throughout the land, and accurate records of rainfall were kept some 200 years before Europeans began such practice. Many astronomical instruments were invented, and scientific experiments for peaceful purposes were conducted under government sponsorship.

Meanwhile, the knowledge of medicine grew and many books on diseases and drugs were published.

Art, Architecture, and Crafts

Although Chinese-style landscape painting dominated the field of painting, scholar-painters and those painters trained at a government School of Art painted flowers, plants, birds and animals as well as portraits. Such plants as pine, bamboo, orchids, plum, and chrysanthemum were favorite subjects for professional and amateur painters. Many fine paintings of cats and dogs were also produced.

Music made great advances under the sponsorship of the Yi court and Confucian shrines. The upper-class enjoyed refined and graceful

Left: Ten-story stone pagoda of the Wongak temple. It is located in the Pagoda Park in Seoul.

Below: *Journey to the Peach Garden* by An Kyon.

Kyŏnghoeru pavilion in the Kyŏngbok palace.

The South Gate of Seoul.

music (*a-ak*) performed by court musicians and dancers. Such musicians as Pak Yŏn of the 15th century produced new instruments and systematized the forms of Chinese music which had been imported as he published many books on music.

The architectural art was represented by grand yet fine palace buildings and pavilions. Most of them were burned down by Japanese invaders of the late 16th century. The survivors included Seoul's South Gate and East Gate.

The architecture of the Yi period reflected the mood and grand design of the Yi dynasty itself. The enormous size of the palaces and government buildings and such buildings as the Kyŏnghoeru pavilion in the Kyŏngbok palace grounds clearly represented the ambitions of the Yi kings.

Portrait of Admiral Yi Sun-sin.

A painting of the scene of Korean soldiers defending Pusan during the 1592-1597 war.

THE FOREIGN INVASIONS AND THE SURMOUNTING OF NATIONAL CRISES

Japanese and Manchu Invasions

Toyotomi Hideyoshi of Japan, who established his mastery over all Japan in 1590 and had a dream of building a vast empire, dispatched in 1592 about 160,000 troops to conquer first Korea and then China. Japanese troops with superior firearms pushed northward from the south coast, and within a month they captured the capital and almost the entire Korean peninsula was under their power.

Admiral Yi Sun-sin, a master tactician who constructed the world's first armored warships called "turtle ships," won tremendous victories against the Japanese in the south seas, and brought about a truce at the end of

The turtle ship.

The seven-year war inflicted severe damages upon Korea. Japanese troops ravaged and despoiled the whole country, destroyed many historic buildings, including palace buildings in Seoul, killed hundreds of thousands of people, took back captive hundreds of potters and skilled workers to Japan, and laid waste to a vast amount of farmlands. It was one of the greatest disasters that struck Korea.

Although a Korean mission was dispatched to Edo, the capital of the Tokugawa Shogunate, in 1811 upon Japanese request, normal relations between Korea and Japan had not been fully restored since the 1592–97 war.

The Manchus, who established their empire named Later Chin in Manchuria, invaded Korea, in 1627 and 1636. The unprepared Yi dynasty succumbed to Manchu demands and accepted the Manchu Empire as its superior.

The wall and gate of Mt. Namhan Fortress where Yi dynasty kings would take refuge during foreign invasion.

The shrine of Admiral Yi Sun-sin.

1593 when the Korean navy under his command cut off supply lines from Japan.

In early 1597, however, the Japanese renewed the fighting by sending a fresh army of 140,000 men to Korea. Meanwhile, Chinese troops of the Ming dynasty arrived in Korea in order to assist the Koreans. The combined forces of Korea and China frustrated Japanese plans. With the death of Toyotomi Hideyoshi at the end of 1597, Japanese invaders withdrew from Korea in disarray.

Opposite page: (Left) Sea battle scene.
(Right) Construction of a turtle ship. By having turtle ships built during the year preceding Japanese invasion in 1592, Admiral Yi Sun-sin prepared for the foreign invasion.
(Bottom) Turtle ship model.

NEW MOVEMENTS IN THE KOREAN SOCIETY

The Arrival of the First Europeans

As the Europeans were penetrating Asia in the 15th and 16th centuries, Koreans who traveled to China came in contact with the Western people. In 1608, maps produced by the Europeans and books written by a Jesuit Father in China, Matteo Ricci, were brought back to Korea. In 1631, the Koreans who visited Ming China established contacts with Catholic missionaries there and brought back books on astronomy, mathematics, geography and cartography, as well as maps, along with telescopes and alarm clocks. With this, knowledge about the West began to grow in Korea.

Korea's direct contacts with Europeans came in 1627 when a Dutchman named Jan Janse Weltevree and two of his companions who came ashore on the south coast were captured. While the ship, which perhaps was engaged in piracy, fled from the Korean waters, the three Dutchmen were kept in Korea to produce weapons and train Korean troops.

In July 1653, a Dutch ship named the *Sparrow Hawk* was shipwrecked near Cheju Island off the southwestern coast of Korea, and Hendrik Hamel and some 30 crew members were rescued by the Koreans. Those Dutchmen too were kept in Korea as spies for a long time. Hamel, who with some of his companions, escaped from Korea published the first book on Korea in 1668 in Holland and introduced Korea to the Europeans.

The Rise of the Sirhak Movement

In the 16th century, a new group of Confucian scholars advocated reforms, and started the *Sirhak* (Practical Learning) movement. *Sirhak* scholars criticized the theoretical arguments which the Neo-Confucian scholars upheld. They advocated the promotion of utilitarian knowledge, political, economic, educational, and economic reforms to promote political morality, social harmony, economic improvement, and educational growth. After the Japanese and Manchuria invasions, the *Sirhak* movement spearheaded the national reconstruction movement. They published books and established schools to train a new breed of scholars. Yi Chung-hwan (1690–1760?) published a book on geography of Korea entitled, *Geographical Description of the Eight Provinces.*

Two illustrations from the Dutchman Hendric Hamel's Description du Royaume de Coree, Amsterdam, 1668; the one is that of his boat drifting and the one depicts his landing on Cheju Island.

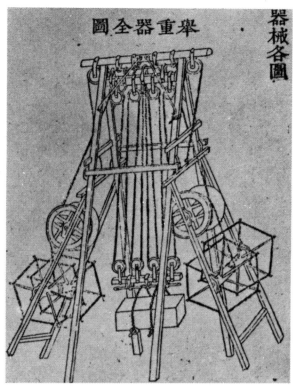

A crane created by Tasan Chŏng Yak-yong.

The Practical Learning movement, which promoted the concepts of rights of man and social equality, continued to grow during the 18th and early 19th centuries. During the height of the *Sirhak* movement in the 18th century, many outstanding scholars emerged. Among them was Chŏng Yak-yong (pen name Tasan), who, like a Renaissance man, studied political, economic, social, religious, medical, and scientific subjects, advocated not only political and social reforms, but also the promotion of education for the people and a land reform to improve the economic conditions of the peasants. He published many books, including a political handbook and a book entitled *On Vaccination for Smallpox.*

Under the Practical Learning movement, new intellectual interests grew and many new fields of studies developed. More books on history including *A History of Ancient Korea* and the *History of Koryŏ,* geography, plants, fish, and medicine along with books on politics, education, and economics were published, and more maps of Korea, including that of Kim Chŏng-ho's map of Korea of 1861 were produced. The spirit of the Practical Learning movement exerted a profound influence on the reform and progressive movements of the late 19th century.

Taedong yŏjido(Map of Korea) by Kim Chŏng-ho. Produced in 1861, it was the most detailed map of Korea.

63

Kyujanggak(Royal Library) and its collection which includes writings by kings.

Village School(sŏdang) by Tanwŏn Kim Hong-do.

The Development of Folk Culture

The deterioration of the *yangban*-dominated society during and after the Japanese and Manchu wars brought about significant new cultural and social trends. Although the *yangban* class as such remained intact, its influence, notably that of its culture, declined much. With this, the folk culture of the common people grew rapidly.

The common people, aided by some educated professional artists, promoted folk culture which they had inherited from their ancestors as they were adding new aspects to it. Folk culture of the Koreans showed freedom and spontaneity which were lacking in the upper-class culture. Folk painting, music, and dance which developed enriched the cultural heritage of the Korean people.

The style of folk painting was unique. Not only the subjects of folk paintings were different, but colors used were distinctively different from others. Most folk paintings were highly decorative in bright colors.

The Korean painters of the 18th century developed new styles of painting, and much like those European painters of the 19th century, they painted different subjects, expressing strong individualism. They created the Korean genre painting, and all their paintings were of Korean scenery or subjects. Chŏng Sŏn was the one who revolutionized the style of landscape painting in his famous painting of Mt. Kŭmgang.

Kim Hong-do (pen name was Tanwŏn), Sin Yun-bok (pen name was Hyewŏn) and Kim Tŭk-sin (pen name was Kŭngjae) of the

64

Wrestling Match by Kim Hong-do.

Right: *Portrait of a Woman* by Sin Yun-bok.

18th century produced marvelous genre
paintings, depicting various scenes of men
and women in action, and hills and streams
in their landscape paintings were those of
Korea.

Although Buddhism was suppressed, the
Buddhist monks established new centers of
Buddhism in remote areas, and built such
beautiful and imposing buildings as the main
halls of the Sŏkwang temple and the Pulguk
temple, and other buildings of the Haein and
the Pŏpchu temples.

The potters of the Yi period produced
beautiful white celadons which were simple
in style, but more spontaneous and original
than the Koryŏ celadons. The white celadon

Women Enjoying at the Creek by Sin Yun-bok.

Men and Girl Enjoying at the Pond by Sin Yun-bok.

Opposite page: *Landscape of Mt. Kŭmgang* by Chŏng Sŏn.

wares of the Yi period with floral and other designs in light blue or brown colors had the beauty and elegance which were admired by the Chinese and the Japanese alike.

The furniture-makers produced highly artistic and decorative furniture for the *yangban* class. The manufacture of brass wares likewise developed rapidly.

One of the most significant cultural aspects of the early Yi period was the participation of women in the cultural movement. To be sure, the number of women who did so was small, but many women of the upper-class, as well as *kisaeng* (female entertainers) became

Breaking the Calm, a genre painting by Kim Tŭk-sin.

Opposite page: White porcelain jar with grapevine design painted in underglaze iron.

active participants in cultural life.

Folk music, including songs, dance, mask and puppet plays became ever popular after the 17th century. The influence of the native religion known as Shamanism in folk music and plays was conspicuous. A large number of folk songs were produced and sung. A new form of dramatic narrative music called *p'ansori* and musical drama called *ch'anggŭk* developed, enriching the cultural life of the

Three-storied wooden book cabinet, 19c.

Hahoe mask.

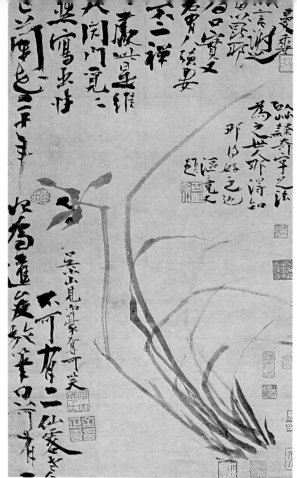

The calligraphy in the Ch'usa style by Wandang Kim Chŏng-hŭi.

commoners, as well as the upper-class people.

Mask dances and puppet plays became valuable cultural properties of the Koreans. Among the most popular mask dances were the Lion Dance.

New calligraphers such as Kim Chŏng-hŭi (pen names were Ch'usa and Wandang) arose and contributed toward the development of Korean culture. They created new styles of calligraphy, expressing strong individualism. Kim Chŏng-hŭi established a new style called Ch'usach'e.

The upper-class poets produced Chinese-style poems called hansi. However, the Korean poetry called sijo, which was created toward the end of the Koryŏ period, grew increasingly popular. The sijo is a short, polished

A secret gathering of the Catholics.

poem, and it was sung to lute accompaniment.

Introduction and Growth of Catholicism

Catholicism was introduced to Korea by a Korean who visited China in 1608, but it did not grow until the 18th century. Catholicism called the Western Learning (*Sŏhak* in Korean) among the *Sirhak* scholars, grew after Yi Sŭng-hun (1756–1801), a scholar who was baptized in Peking in 1783, returned to Korea with many religious books. It was he who established the foundation for Catholicism in Korea despite the opposition of the government and the *yangban* class. Among many *Sirhak* scholars who became Catholics and involved in the Western Learning was Tasan Chŏng Yak-yong.

The government promulgated anti-Catholic edicts in 1791 and after, and began to persecute the Catholics. Despite the government actions against Catholicism, the new religion grew, and in 1831 the Korean diocese was established. In 1838–37 after, more French priests, including Pierre P. Maubant entered Korea. The persecution of 1839 and 1846 produced more martyrs, including a Korean Father Kim Tae-gŏn (Andrew Kim, 1822–1846), but they could not stamp out Catholicism which had taken deep roots in Korea.

Anti-Catholic policy was relaxed in 1849

Execution of the Catholics, including some French priests.

French bishop and fathers who were executed in 1866.

Statue of Father Kim Tae-gŏn.

with accession of King Ch'ŏljong, and the number of Catholic converts grew to 11,000 in 1850 and to 23,000 by 1865, with the arrival of more French priests, including Father Berneux. The agitation against Catholicism grew strong after the accession of King Kojong in 1864 and when his father became the regent to his young son. The Regent Taewŏn'gun carried out a bloody anti-Catholic move in 1866, and made some 8,000 martyrs, including the death of several French missionaries.

The Rise of the Tonghak Sect

In around 1860, Ch'oe Che-u (1824–1864), a descendant of a fallen *yangban* family, established a new religion called the *Tonghak* (The Eastern Learning). With this, the *Tonghak* movement began. It was against the corrupt government and its officials, social injustice, the privileged *yangban* class, and the Western Learning, i.e., the Catholicism.

The aims of the founder of the *Tonghak* sect were to rescue the suffering masses spiritually as well as physically. While he preached the gospel of the new religion, he also advocated political, social, and economic reforms. The most important concept which he advanced was the unity of god and man, or "man is god." Such a revolutionary concept created an entirely new value and dignity of man.

In view of the rising influence of teaching of Ch'oe, the government outlawed the *Tonghak* and executed Ch'oe in 1864. However, the *Tonghak* movement grew under the leadership of his successor, Ch'oe Si-hyŏng.

A memorial monument erected on the cliff in Yanghwajin of the Han River in honor of 8,000 Koreans who lost their lives for their religion.

4 CHALLENGES OF MODERNIZATION: REFORM AND INDEPENDENCE MOVEMENTS

The Korean people encountered new challenges in the 19th century as the world was shrinking and western powers were encroaching in Asia. Since Korea had no relations with the West, western nations called Korea a "hermit kingdom." But, Korea could not remain a secluded nation, and eventually the pressure that was brought upon Korea by Japan and the western powers led to the opening of Korea, establishing modern relations with them toward the end of the 19th century. With this, Korea encountered a variety of problems as the need for her to become modern and preserve her sovereignty and territorial integrity grew. In response to new challenges, the reform and independence movement of the Koreans rose.

The Opening of Korea

The Japanese in 1868 proposed the establishment of normal relations between Korea and Japan. The reluctance of the Korean government to do so, and its mishandling of Japanese envoys provided a convenient excuse for some aggressive Japanese to advocate a war against Korea in the early 1870s.

Korea had already encountered serious

From Ernest Oppert's book on Korea, *Forbidden Land*, an illustration of steamer *Emperor* at anchor at Kanghwa Island.

military threats from France, and the United States following the execution of French priests in 1866 and the destruction of an American merchant ship, the *General Sherman,* on the Taedong River near P'yŏngyang and the killing of its captain and crew in the summer of 1866. In October 1866, a French fleet invaded Korea and had a brief war with her on Kanghwa Island and in the area between Seoul and Chemulp'o (now Inch'ŏn). In May 1871, American Marines invaded Korea and fought a short war on Kanghwa Island and in the area where French troops had fought a short time ago. The French and American attempts made to attack the capital were blocked by Korean troops, although hundreds of Korean troops were killed.

The two foreign invasions of Korea, together with the tomb-robbing expeditions of Ernest Oppert, a German who was a naturalized U.S. citizen, led the Regent Taewŏn'gun to officially declare the policy of isolation in 1871, but challenges from Japan and western nations did not stop, as more foreign ships violated

Ch'ojijin, Kanghwa Island.

A weaponry displayed at Kanghwa Island, the target of naval assaults by the French in 1866 and again by the Americans in 1871.

Opposite page: (Above) American troops, who took over Ch'ojijin fortress on Kanghwa Island, under Commander C.A. Kimberley.
(Below) Hqs. of Commodore Rogers (seated at center).

Above left: Regent Taewŏngun.
Above right: A stone tablet on which anti-western policy was inscribed. The inscription said, "Western barbarians have invaded our land. If we do not fight and conclude peace with them, it will lead to the selling of the country to them." Stone tablets with this inscription were placed throughout the country.

the territorial rights of Korea. However, in 1873, the nationalistic Taewŏn'gun was forced to retire because of a financial crisis which he brought about in connection with the coining of a new money and the reconstruction of palace building in the Kyŏngbok palace which had been burned down by the Japanese in the 1592–97 war. The young king came under the domination of Queen Min and her supporters.

While the Russians persisted in establishing trade with Korea from the 1850s, the Japanese became more warlike and aggressive toward Korea between 1869 and 1875. Then in 1875, the Japanese government sent a warship to Pusan in the southeastern corner of Korea, and intimidated the Koreans there. After

that, the Japanese warship went to Kanghwa Island and provoked the Korean troops on the island.

A fleet of Japanese warships invaded Korea in February 1876. Arriving at Kanghwa Island, the commander of the fleet and a Japanese envoy threatened the Korean government as they demanded that a treaty be signed between Korea and Japan to establish diplomatic and commercial relations between the two countries. The Japanese made it clear that if Korea refused, they would start a war. Under such a threat of the Japanese, who acted like the westerners who opened China and Japan in similar manner, the Korean government signed the Kanghwa Treaty in February 1876 with Japan.

Unyo, the Japanese warship which invaded Korea in 1875.

Sometime after Japan forced Korea to establish new diplomatic and commercial relations with her, western powers, particularly the United States became more interested in opening Korea for them to have diplomatic and commercial relations with the "hermit kingdom." The efforts made by the United States government either directly or through Japanese mediation to achieve its aims did not succeed.

The first treaty of friendship and commerce between the United States and Korea (commonly called the Shufeldt Treaty or the Chemulp'o Treaty) was established on May 22, 1882 at Chemulp'o (now Inch'ŏn). How-

The treaty negotiation between the Korean and the Japanese representatives at Kanghwa.

Chemulp'o at the time when the U.S.-Korean treaty was signed. Now Inch'ŏn.

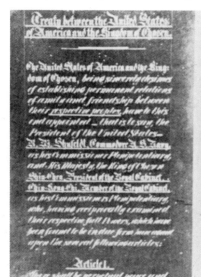

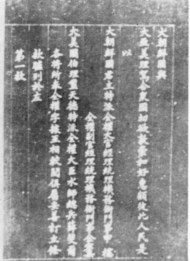

The Chemulp'o Treaty of May 22, 1882 in Chinese and English.

First U.S. minister Lucius Foote.

ever Li Hung-chang failed to induce the United States to recognize China's suzerainty over Korea. Following this, Korea signed similar treaties with other western nations, thus ending her policy of isolation.

After the conclusion of treaties with Japan and the United States, the Korean government sent missions to Japan in 1881 and to the United States in 1883 to learn more about these countries and promote friendly relations. Western influence began to grow slowly in Korea with the arrival of western diplomats, advisers, and missionaries to Korea.

THE PROGRESSIVE MOVEMENT

Many members of the missions sent to Japan and the United States brought back startling information about them. The young scholars who went to these countries were impressed with advanced systems and national strength of Japan and America. They became enlightened and felt the urgency for Korea to change and modernize her systems, and promote national strength.

The objectives of the Progressives were to modernize the government, develop the econo-

A parade of the Korean mission to Japan headed by Kim Ki-su.

The first Korean goodwill mission of Korea sent to the United States in 1883.

my, promote education and culture, and bring about social progress, including social equality. Above all, they wanted to establish an unquestioned national independence by making Korea free from Chinese interference.

They were able to induce the government to employ in 1881 a Japanese military instructor to train Korean troops with modern weapons and military tactics, send a mission to the United States with a hurriedly created national flag (current national flag of the Republic of Korea) and with credentials written only in *han'gŭl* in 1883. In cooperation with the American minister to Korea, Lucius H. Foote, they were able to induce the government to establish a palace school and employ American teachers, as well as an American military adviser. King Kojong established a modern farm with seeds and cattle which were brought back by the first Korean mission to the United States. The modern postal service system was adopted, and in 1884 the

Korean Consulate in Washington D.C. established by Pak Chŏng-yang, the first Korean minister to U.S.A. in June 1887.

Korean soldiers in western-style uniform.

King Kojong.

Queen Min.

Modern military training for Korean troops.

first post office opened its business.

However, reactionary and conservative Confucian government officials who were allied with Queen Min saw potential political challenges to them and the queen, and they attempted to block the nationalistic progressive movement of the reform advocates who were also anti-Chinese. Consequently, a serious conflict between the Progressives and their opponents developed, particularly after the Chinese military intervention in Korean internal affairs of the summer of 1882. In July 1882, the Chinese government sent troops to Korea to crush an anti-Chinese, anti-Queen Min military insurrection of ex-Regent Taewŏn'gun, and taking Taewŏn'gun to China as a prisoner, the Chinese put Queen Min in charge of the government. King Kojong was helpless.

Seeing the growing danger to national independence with the increasing Chinese domination in Korea, and sensing a strong urgency for modernization of Korea, the Progressives carried out a coup d'état known

Portrait of Kim Ok-kyun, a progressive movement leader.

The first post office building opened in 1884.

as *Kapsin chŏngbyŏn* in December 1884 and established a reform government under King Kojong in cooperation with the Japanese. Immediately after this, the new government adopted a new national policy to strengthen national sovereignty, and to bring about political, economic, educational and social reforms in order to make Korea a modern and progressive nation.

The Chinese again sent troops to Korea in December 1884, and in collusion with the reactionaries in Korea, they overthrew the reform government. The Chinese again put Queen Min and her supporters who were pro-Chinese in charge of the government. Thus, the Chinese robbed Korea of a golden opportunity to become a modern nation and protect her sovereignty and territorial integrity at a critical juncture in her history.

In 1885, Korea faced a serious international complication when British troops without the consent of the Korean government occupied a Korean island named Kŏmundo off the south coast. Russia quickly threatened to take over Korean territory in retaliation of the British occupation of the Korean territory. The Anglo-Russian rivalries in the Balkan region and in the Middle East were now about to involve Korea into a conflict between two European powers. However the British withdrew from Kŏmun Island, and the threat of a war between two foreign powers in Korea subsided.

Tombstone of British soldier in Kŏmun Island.

THE DEVELOPMENT OF MODERN EDUCATION AND CHRISTIANITY

With the establishment of religious freedom, Christianity grew much. The American missionaries of the Methodist and Presbyterian mission boards, such as Drs. Homer B. Hulbert, Henry G. Appenzeller, Horace G. Underwood, and Mrs. Mary F. Scranton, contributed much to the development of modern education in Korea.

The first modern school was Yŏngyuk hakwŏn, a palace school where American teachers taught sons of aristocrats, which was established in 1883. In 1885, the American Presbyterian mission in Korea established the first school named Paejae for boys, and in 1886, the Methodist mission established the first modern school named Ewha for girls, thus opening the doors for the children of commoners and others to receive the new education.

More schools for boys and girls were subsequently established by American missionaries. Meanwhile, private schools which were established by Korean nationalists emerged. Among them were Posŏng (now Korea University), Yangjŏng and Hwimun for boys, and Sukmyŏng and Chinmyŏng for girls.

English language school for Koreans established by American missionaries.

Paejae school, the first modern educational institution in Korea, 1886.

Portrait of Henry G. Appenzeller.

Christianity spread rapidly as a modernizing influence. Although it was rejected by conservative Confucian *yangban* people as a whole, many of them, as well as the commoners became Christians. The Protestant missionaries of various denominations not only taught their religion, but they also established hospitals, schools, printing presses, and conducted lectures on various secular subjects, including agriculture, commerce, and industry. Through their teachings, the concept of freedom, rights and equality grew among the Koreans as new cultural trends developed. Meanwhile, American and Canadian medical doctors made a significant contribution toward the growth of medical knowledge as hospitals which they established provided better medical care to millions of Koreans.

A class of Ewha Girls' School.

A building of Ewha Girls' School in 1887.

Chinese troops sent to Korea to suppress the *Tonghak* rebels.

REVOLUTION, WAR AND THE KAPO REFORM

The Tonghak Revolution

The *Tonghak* sect which arose in the middle of the 19th century steadily grew despite actions taken by the government against it because of worsening economic and social conditions of the people who had strong resentments against the government, the upper-class; and corrupted officials.

In February 1894, Chŏn Pong-jun, a radical leader of *Tonghak*, initiated a revolt against a local magistrate, and fighting between the *Tonghak* rebels and government troops began. Soon after this, the believers of the *Tonghak* religion in other parts of Korea rose up against the government. The Revolution began.

The *Tonghak* forces defeated government troops everywhere and occupied the capital of Chŏlla province. They threatened to attack the capital when their appeals to the Yi government were rejected. Facing the threat in June, the government made concessions to the representatives of the *Tonghak* leaders

Chŏn Pong-jun, a radical rebel leader of the *Tonghak* rebellion, taken prison in November 1894.

and a truce was established. Meanwhile, the Korean government asked China for help against the revolutionaries.

The Sino-Japanese War

When the *Tonghak* revolution took place, the Japanese concluded that sooner or later the Korean government would ask China for

Japanese troops landed at Inch'ŏn.

help and the Chinese would send troops to Korea. Under this assumption, the Japanese adopted various war plans with a conviction that only a war with China would remove Chinese control over Korea and prevent Korea from falling into the hands of western powers, particularly those of Russia.

Shortly after the arrival of Chinese troops and a fleet of warships to Korea in early June 1894, 500 Japanese Marines arrived and entered the capital, followed by over 20,000 Japanese troops.

Both Chinese and Japanese commanders refused to withdraw their troops from Korea, despite the request made by the Korean government. The Sino-Japanese War began on July 25. During the war, the combined forces of Korea and Japan destroyed the *Tonghak* revolutionaries.

The Japanese won a quick victory. The Chinese recognized Korea as a sovereign and independent nation, but Korea had fallen under the complete domination of the Japanese. The Korean government signed many agreements with the Japanese, increasing Japanese influence in Korea.

Chinese troops in Lushun preparing for a decisive final battle.

Chinese commanders surrender to the Japanese.

84

Trial scene before legal reform.

A modern court.

Whipping of an accused.

Police uniform before legal reform.

The Kapo Reform

During the Sino-Japanese War, the Japanese brought heavy pressures on the Korean government and King Kojong to institute structural and financial reforms. Meanwhile, the Korean leaders came to a realization that something had to be done by themselves to save the country. Thus, came the *Kapo* Reform of the 1894–96 period.

The *Kapo* Reform abolished the old Confucian civil service system opening the doors of the government to talented people regardless of their birth, bringing the decline of the power of the *yangban* class to a certain degree. A judicial reform introduced the modern court system and a new police system. It also freed public slaves and forbade the sale of slaves.

The Rise of Russo-Japanese Rivalry and War

The Triple Intervention of Russia, Germany and France, which forced Japan to cancel the agreement for the leasing of the Liaotung peninsula in the southwestern corner of Manchuria from China which was included in the Shimonoseki Treaty of April 1895, brought about a sudden decline of Japanese influence in Korea. The concession made by Japan to Russia and others was regarded by the Koreans as a sign of weakness. With this, the influence of Russia grew in Korea. The pro-Japanese government fell, replaced by a pro-Russian cabinet.

New uniformed policemen.

Japanese artillery unit passing through Korea.

Russian artillery brigade troops.

King Kojong was forced to reside at the Russian Legation for a year, and during his residence there Russian influence grew strong over the Korean government as Russia and other western nations, including the United States, gained many concessions from Korea.

Meanwhile, a Korean delegate to Russia to attend the coronation ceremony of Tsar Nicholas II concluded secret agreements with Russia in 1896, and Russian financial and military advisers arrived in Korea to be followed by a large number of Russian military instructors. In 1896, Russia rejected a Japanese proposal to divide Korea into two spheres of interests between Russia and Japan along the 39th parallel line.

Peace conference at Portsmouth; Japan gained control over Korea with the signing of the Portsmouth Treaty.

Japanese victory at sea. The Baltic fleet of Russia was demolished in the Korea Strait.

Yun Ch'i-ho.

Yi Sung-man

THE RISE OF REFORM SOCIETIES AND A NEW CULTURE MOVEMENT

When Korea became an arena for international diplomatic contests for concessions, and her existence as an independent nation became precarious, many nationalistic individuals and societies emerged along with a new culture movement to reconstruct the Korean society and rejuvenate its people.

The Independence Club

Among many societies which emerged and advocated nationalism and reform measures was the Independence Club which arose in 1896. The leading advocates for nationalism and reform were Yun Ch'i-ho, Yi Sang-jae, Yi Sŭng-man (Syngman Rhee) and Sŏ Chae-p'il (Philip Jaisohn).

It established a press and published a Korean language newspaper named *The Independent* from April 1896, with which they promoted the spirit of nationalism and independence, progressivism and enlightenment of the people, and advocated economic and social reforms. The Independence Club was strongly against Korea's reliance on foreign powers for her own security and well-being, and it conducted numerous public lectures and held public rallies. They brought about the dismantling of the old "Welcome Gate" for the Chinese emissaries in Seoul in 1896, and the Independence Arch was constructed on its spot.

The Independence Arch.

A copy of *The Independent* and So Chae-p'il.

New Culture Movement

In conjunction with the national independence movement, the voice of reformers grew loud as new cultural trends developed bringing a new cultural movement for the enlightenment of the people.

Realizing that enlightenment of the people and social progress were urgently needed to enhance national independence as well as the spirit of independence among the people, the nationalists formed various societies to promote modern education and they established primary and secondary schools. Thus, between 1897 and 1909, 25 private secondary schools emerged. Seven of them were those of American mission boards, which had already established four schools before 1897. By 1909 the number of private modern schools had grown to 3,000. The growth of the number of modern schools, along with Korean language newspapers and magazines, increased the usage of *han'gŭl* (Korean script). Both *The Independent,* the organ of the Independence Club, and the Bible, as well as Christian hymnals and religious materials were published in Korean. Although Chinese characters were used in printing books, magazines, and newspapers, including the government publications, the writing in Korean language grew steadily, contributing to the decline of illiteracy.

New literary figures arose and promoted a new cultural movement for enlightenment. They advanced the concepts of the spirit of independence of both the nation and individuals as well as the equality of man and sexual equality. They preached the discarding of superstition, family reform, marriage reform, and the reconstruction of the Korean society.

Smallpox vaccination had been imported in 1897, a modern hospital was established and the first post office was opened in 1884, in 1893 telegraph and telephone systems, electrical lamps, and street car lines were installed in 1898 in Seoul, and the railway line between Seoul and Inch'ŏn was constructed by an American firm. Meanwhile, many new institutions were established, such as the Bank of Korea, and western-style architecture began to appear. These developments contributed much toward the modernization of Korea.

Sub-editors at work on *The Independent* in 1890s.

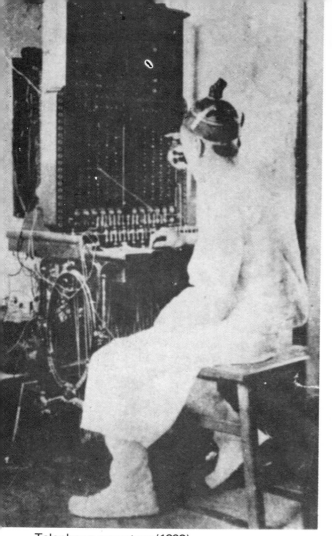
Telephone operators (1893).

Type pickers of *The Independent*.

The Bank of Korea building.

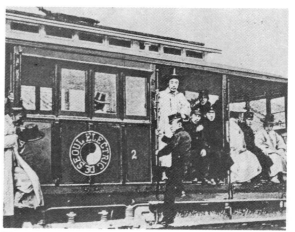
The early street car in Korea (1893).

5 THE JAPANESE SEIZURE OF KOREA AND THE FIGHT FOR FREEDOM

THE JAPANESE SEIZURE OF KOREA

In 1905, Japan seized Korea and made her into a semi-colony, and in 1910, the Japanese annexed Korea and ruled Korea as their full-fledged colony until August 1945. During this long period of Japanese domination Koreans at home and abroad continued their fight for freedom of their country.

The Russo-Japanese struggle over Korea and Manchuria grew intense between 1901, and 1903. In 1903, it reached a dangerous point when all efforts made by Japan to settle the question with Russia failed. The offer made by Japan to recognize Manchuria as Russia's exclusive sphere of interest if Russia

acknowledged Korea as an exclusive sphere of interests of Japan was rejected.

Following the conclusion of the Anglo-Japanese Alliance in 1902, the Japanese became more aggressive toward Russia, and when Russia refused to negotiate with them further, they delivered an ultimatum in late 1903 to Russia. When Russia refused the Japanese offer, Japan declared war on Russia in February 1904.

A large number of Japanese troops invaded Korea and Manchuria. Korea was again occupied by Japanese troops, and during the Russo-Japanese War the Korean govern-

90

ment was forced to sign many agreements with the Japanese. With these agreements, the Japanese established their control over the Korean government as they secured many more privileges in Korea.

In the Portsmouth Treaty of September 1905 which ended the Russo-Japanese War, both Japan and Russia acknowledged the independence of Korea, but the Japanese established a protectorateship over Korea with the support of Great Britain and the United States. Whereas Great Britain supported the Japanese move in Korea with the Anglo-Japanese Alliance of 1902, U.S. President Theodore Roosevelt concluded a secret understanding with the Japanese and gave a green light to the Japanese to put Korea under their control. Roosevelt even suggested to the Japanese that Japan ought to take over Korea completely.

Korea, abandoned by Great Britain and the United States, could not withstand Japanese threats and the Japanese militarists forced the Korean emperor to sign the Treaty of Protection on November 17, 1905. Following this, the Japanese established the Residency-General in Korea and ruled. Between 1905 and 1907, the Japanese abolished the Ministry of Foreign Affairs of Korea and the Korean Army. The Japanese began to appropriate Korean land as they brought more Japanese to Korea.

Emperor Kojong made fruitless efforts to regain Korea's sovereignty and independence by soliciting the assistance of the United States and other western powers. He dispatched missions to the United States in 1905, and in 1907 he sent a mission headed by Yi Sang-sŏl and Yi Chun to the Hague Peace Conference to let western powers know that he signed the 1905 treaty under duress and military threats of the Japanese, and therefore, it was null and void. At the same time, his mission sought to receive help from

Photographs of emissaries inset in a newspaper in the Hague and other clippings of the news of their activities in that city at that time.

Tomb of Yi Chun in Seoul.

Portrait of Min Yŏng-hwan.

Crown Prince Yŏngch'in (son of Emperor Sunjong) and Ito Hirobumi who became his "guardian." The Prince was taken to Japan under Ito's custody.

Prince Yŏngch'in, Prime Minister Yi Wan-yong and his Cabinet ministers.

Interrogation of An Chung-gŭn at Lushun prison.

Ito's party at Harbin railway station platform.

western powers to remove the Japanese control from Korea.

Some patriotic Koreans including a nobleman named Min Yŏng-hwan, committed suicide in protest while Korean newspapers, such as the *Capital News* (*Hwangsŏng sinmun*) of Chang Chi-yŏn bitterly criticized the actions taken by the Japanese. A strong popular protest against the Japanese encroachment rose. Meanwhile the Righteous Armies of 141,600 men emerged and fought 2,819 battles against the Japanese until 1909, but they could not save the nation from the Japanese. Many Confucian scholars, such as Min Chong-sik and Ch'oe Ik-hyŏn, organized the Righteous Armies joined by former military officers and men, as well as peasants.

Facing these, the Japanese forced Emperor Kojong to abdicate in July 1907, and after putting Sunjong on the throne as their puppet, the Japanese proceeded to strengthen their control over Korea.

In 1908, a Korean student in San Francisco assassinated Durham White Stevens, who was an adviser to the Korean government but secretly conspired with the Japanese, and in October 1909 another patriot named An Chung-gŭn shot and killed Ito Hirobumi, the first Resident-General in Korea in Harbin, Manchuria, but they could not stop the Japanese from carrying out their plan. Emperor Sunjong was powerless to resist the Japanese pressure and threats. The Korean government signed the Treaty of Annexation on August 22, 1910. With this the Yi dynasty of 27 rulers which ruled Korea for 519 years ceased to exist.

JAPANESE COLONIAL RULE

The Government-General Building, the symbol of Japanese colonialism.

Government and Policy

When Japan annexed Korea, the Japanese emperor stated in his Imperial Rescript of 1910 that the Koreans will be treated as Japanese subjects. But, the Japanese established a colonial government called the Government-General of Korea and ruled Korea as their colony. All Governors-General, except one, were Army generals who exercised judicial, legislative, and administrative power, and they were empowered to mobilize Japanese troops in Korea.

Under the militaristic rule, the freedom of speech, press, and assembly of the Koreans was taken away, many private schools and all Korean language newspaper presses were closed down, the teaching of Korean history was banned, and the nationalist movement and anti-Japanese activities were strictly forbidden. Hundreds of patriotic Koreans were imprisoned within a short period of time, and prisons were over-flowing with Korean political prisoners.

Thousands of Japanese farmers were brought to Korea, and they received free lands or bought farm land at a low price. With this, some 2 million Koreans became tenant farmers.

The main economic policy of the Japanese was to make Korea an agricultural colony, producing more food grains and raw materials for Japan. A large portion of rice produced in Korea was exported to Japan, creating a serious shortage of food in Korea.

The Japanese did not promote education in Korea or train Koreans to be professionals, technicians, scientists, or skilled workers. The primary educational objective of the Japanese was to make the Koreans loyal, obedient, and useful subjects of the Japanese emperor. To be sure, the number of primary and secondary schools grew steadily, but unlike in Japan, there was no compulsory primary education in Korea.

The March First Movement

The Koreans who suffered oppressive and humiliating treatment at the hands of the Japanese during the decade of 1910–1919, desperately wanted opportunities to come for them to regain their freedom and restore national independence. Even in the darkest period in Korean history, the Koreans refused to abandon their hopes as they struggled against all odds.

When American President Woodrow Wilson enunciated his Fourteen Points, in which the principle of self-determination of subjugated peoples was included, the hopes of the Koreans became high.

The leaders of the Korean independence movement in Korea adopted a plan to have a nationwide demonstration on March 1, expressing the desire of the Korean people to be free and independent from Japan. Thirty-three Korean nationalists signed the Korean Declaration of Independence.

The bronze mural at Pagoda Park commemorates the March 1 Movement when Korean patriots demonstrated for independence here.

Patriot Son Pyŏng-hui.

Girl students in the March 1 Movement.

On March 1, the Declaration of Independence was read everywhere and public rallies were held. Some two million Korean people participated in the peaceful demonstration against the Japanese, and they made it absolutely clear that they did not wish to remain under oppressive Japanese colonial rule. The shout, "Long Live Korean Independence" was heard throughout Korea.

Japan's response to Korean's independence movement was immediate and brutal. The Japanese gendarmerie and policy killed 25,000 Koreans, wounded tens of thousands, burned down thousands of Korean homes and Christian church buildings, and imprisoned some 50,000 Korean patriots. A 17-year old girl student named Yu Kwan-sun, like Joan of Arc in France was brutally murdered by Japanese police, but she planted a stronger patriotism among young Korean students with her blood.

Many Korean nationalists were forced to flee from their fatherland, and they joined

Yu Kwan-sun as a prisoner.

Leaders of the Provisional Government of Korea in exile.

Men of the Korean National Restoration Corps.

Military training of Koreans in the United States.

their compatriots in Shanghai and elsewhere. In April 1919, Korean nationalists in Shanghai established the Provisional Government of the Republic of Korea in exile, and elected Dr. Syngman Rhee, who was leading a Korean nationalist movement in the United States, as its first president.

When World War II broke out, the Provisional Government of Korea declared war on Japan, and collaborated with the Chinese Nationalists as well as allies against the Japanese. The Korean Army for National Restoration in China fought the Japanese aggressors in China in cooperation with anti-Japanese forces.

The contingent of the Korean Army for National Restoration with British troops in Burma during World War II.

Nationalist Movements in Korea after 1919

While Korean nationalists in China, Siberia, the United States, as well as in Japan relentlessly carried out Korea's fight for freedom, the nationalists of rightist and leftist orientations formed various social organizations to maintain the independence movement. As a result, such societies as the New Shoot Society of men and the Society of Friends of Rose of Sharon (Korean national flower) of women, along with many student organization emerged.

Brutal measures taken by the Japanese policy against the Koreans eventually brought about the dissolution of patriotic societies, and Christian churches, particularly those which refused to participate in the Shinto shrine ceremonies, were closed down. Many Christian ministers and others were imprisoned because of their refusal to cooperate with the Japanese.

The Nationalist Movement in Manchuria

In Manchuria, troops of the Korean Army for National Restoration, which was formed by General Kim Chwa-jin, were engaged in military actions against Japanese troops and police in the Kando region, as well as those in the Korean border areas. In 1921, detachments of the Army for National Restoration entered into Korea and clashed with Japanese military and police and won a major victory, killing some 3,300 Japanese.

Many Japanese notables were assassinated or wounded by the Koreans abroad. The assassination attempt on the Japanese emperor by a Korean patriot in 1932 did not succeed, but it, along with other attempts made by

President Kim Ku, and Yun Pong-gil. On April 29, 1932, Yun threw bombs at the Japanese who held birthday celebration for Japanese emperor in a park in Shanghai.

A village of Korean emigrants in Kando, Manchuria.

Korean farmers who emigrated to the United States.

the Koreans clearly demonstrated that the spirit of independence of the Koreans was alive and strong and that Japanese policy and plans failed to win the Korean people.

THE END OF JAPANESE COLONIAL RULE

Japanese aggression in Manchuria in September 1931, followed by their aggression in mainland China in July 1937, made Japanese rule in Korea even tighter. All Korean organizations with the slightest anti-Japanese sentiments were broken up, and the thought control system was strengthened. No freedom of speech and press was given to the Koreans after the March First Movement of 1919, and the three leading Korean language newspapers had all but disappeared by 1939.

With the acceleration of the Japanization program that began in 1936, Korean language instruction was abolished altogether, the speaking of Japanese language was forced upon the people, more Christian schools and churches were closed down, and the attendance at Shinto shrine ceremonies became mandatory. The Koreans were even forced to change their family and given names and adopt Japanese-style family and given names.

As the war in China protracted, and when World War II began, the Japanese became more desperate. More food grains and more raw materials were forced to be produced and more taxes were imposed on the people.

A Korean freedom fighter in Manchuria and weapons used.

Hundreds of thousands Korean workers were mobilized and shipped to Japanese coal mines.

Meanwhile, the Japanese inaugurated in Korea special Army and Navy volunteer systems in 1938, and thousand of Korean youth were sent to battle fields in China and elsewhere. Some 5,000 Korean college and university students in Japan were drafted into the Japanese military since 1943.

When the Japanese emperor accepted on August 15, 1945 the Potsdam Ultimatum of unconditional surrender of July 1945, Japanese colonial rule in Korea ended, and at last Korea's fight for freedom from Japanese was over, and the victory of the Allies brought about the liberation of Korea from Japanese colonial yoke, which the Koreans had awaited for thirty-six years.

6 THE BIRTH OF THE REPUBLIC OF KOREA

THE PARTITION AND FOREIGN OCCUPATION OF KOREA

The Cairo Declaration of December 1943 of the Allies (Great Britain, China and the United States) stated that Korea will be freed from Japan and she will be an independent nation "in due course." Although, U.S. President Franklin D. Roosevelt had a different plan for Korea, the Koreans interpreted the meaning of "in due course" as "when the Pacific War ended and the Japanese were removed from Korea." The Koreans were destined to taste a bitter cup with the U.S. plan to divide the Korean peninsula along the 38th parallel into two military

Korean national flag flies high in the clear sky.

operational zones of the U.S. and U.S.S.R., and occupy Korea. Moreover, it was not the plan of the U.S. to make Korea an independent nation immediately after her liberation from Japan. President Roosevelt wanted to put Korea under the trusteeship of the Allies for a considerable period (up to 35 years) of time after her liberation from Japan.

General John R. Hodge, Commander of U.S. forces in Korea, organized the United States Army Military Government and put South Korea under American military rule. The Koreans were disappointed and became angry, and the warm feelings of the Koreans toward the U.S. quickly cooled off.

People in Seoul rejoice at the news of Liberation
on August 15, 1

Above: People in Seoul rejoice at the news of
Liberation on August 15, 1945.

Below: U.S. troops arrive at the Government-
General building.

THE MOSCOW PLAN AND THE FAILURE OF THE ALLIES

What aroused Korean resentment against the Allies was the Moscow Agreement of December, 1945. The Allied Powers met in Moscow and adopted a plan to form the U.S.–U.S.S.R. Joint Commission, and it was to form a Korean government and put it under a 5-year trusteeship of the Allies. Such a plan was regarded by the Koreans as an insult to 25 million Koreans who fought for their freedom and the restoration of national independence for 36 years.

There was a nation-wide protest against the Moscow Agreement, but in early 1946 the Korean Communists in both north and south Korea changed their minds, and supported the Moscow Agreement under Soviet pressure. Some 2 million Koreans fled from the north to the south for freedom.

During the period of 1946 and 1948, the Soviet authorities rendered positive assistance to a Communist Kim Il-sŏng, and Kim, who came to Korea with Soviet troops, became a Soviet puppet but a strong man in the north. After crushing all nationalist organizations, Kim became the head of a temporary Korean government in Korea under Soviet supervision. Under the tutelage of the Soviet Union, Kim brought about the communization of North Korea.

During the American rule, democratic principles were introduced in South Korea, but soldiers were poor promoters of democracy. However, democracy exercised by the Americans allowed the emergence of political and social organizations, including those of the Communists. When the Korean Communist Party, which changed its name to the South Korean Workers' Party, instigated labor strikes, printed counterfeit money, and engaged in other illegal activities, the American Military Government suppressed the Com-

Anti-trusteeship demonstration.

munists at first, and then forced them to escape to the north later. But, many Communists went underground, and continued to cause a variety of political problems and economic difficulties in the south.

The Koreans went to work under the leadership of Dr. Syngman Rhee and other leaders of the Provisional Government of Korea in exile, who returned to Korea in the fall of 1945 from China and the United States. Despite a temporary set back, the Koreans made determined efforts to prepare for a better future for an independent Korea.

THE ESTABLISHMENT OF THE REPUBLIC OF KOREA

Facing an impasse, the United States government appealed to the United Nations in September 1947, and the General Assembly of the U. N. adopted a resolution in November to form and send the United Nations Temporary Commission on Korea (UNTCOK) to Korea to conduct national elections and establish a Korean government to end the foreign occupation of Korea.

The vast majority of the Koreans wished to see the end of foreign occupation of their fatherland as quickly as possible, and supported the U.N. plan. However when the UNTCOK faced a dilemma, some nationalists such as Dr. Rhee and his supporters advocated the holding of elections in the south first and established a Korean government under U.N. supervision. They had hoped that elections could be held in the north later, and put the north under the government established by the U.N. But, many other nationalists, as well as Communists in the south, vehemently opposed such a plan, fearing that it would lead to a permanent division of the country.

In order to accomplish its mission, the UNTCOK carried out national elections on May 10, 1948. On August 15, 1948, the Republic of Korea was inaugurated, and Dr. Rhee took the oath of office as the first president of the Republic of Korea. With this, American occupation of South Korea ended.

Meanwhile, North Korean Communists carried out their own plan, and under the tutelage of the Soviet Union Kim Il-sung established the so-called Democratic People's Republic in September, with 55% (48,240 sq. miles or 122,370 sq. km.) of the Korean peninsula as its territory, and became its head. Thus the 38th parallel became the Berlin Wall in Korea.

Dr. Rhee taking the oath of office.

Inauguration ceremony for the government of the Republic of Korea.

Peaceful Korean farm village in autumn.

The Republic of Korea, launched in a turbulent sea, weathered violent storms in its early stage. The first was the north Korean Communist-inspired military insurrection of late 1948 and early 1949, and then the Korean War of 1950–53, which the North Korean Communists launched against the Republic in June 1950. These two tragic events determined the political character of the First Republic which lasted until April 1960.

THE KOREAN WAR

Despite the request made by the Korean government to the United States to keep its troops in Korea longer, the United States forces were withdrawn by late summer of 1949, leaving poorly trained and inadequately equipped Korean armed forces of 96,000 men to defend their national independence under some 500 American military advisers. The Soviet Union, on the other hand, gave a large amount of up-to-date military equipment, including 200 jet fighters and 500 heavy tanks, before it withdrew its troops from the north. South Korea had none of these. Moreover, some 2,500 Soviet military advisers remained in the north to train some 175,000 Communist troops there. By June 1950, the number of troops in the north grew to 200,000. With growing military strength and supported by the Soviet Union, North Korea increased its threats to overthrow the Republic in the south.

Above: North Korean aggressors in Seoul with Russian tank.
Right: The U.N. Command is born. General MacArthur receives the U.N. flag.

On January 12, 1950, Secretary of State Dean Acheson disclosed in his speech given at the National Press Club in Washington, D.C. that South Korea was outside the U.S. defense primeter which ran from the Aleutians to the Philippines via Japan. It was seen as a green signal by the north Korean Communists. On early Sunday, June 25, 1950, North Korean troops opened fire and launched a well planned war against South Korea.

North Korean troops, spearheaded by Soviet-made heavy tanks, crossed the 38th parallel, and within four days they captured the South Korean capital of Seoul and over-ran two-thirds of South Korea within a short period of time.

The North Korean attack prompted American President Harry S. Truman to send some American troops back to Korea from Japan, but they were unable to stop the

War refugees push on.

U.S. troops make a surprise-landing at Inch'ŏn.

Gen. MacArthur at his command post on the flag ship.

advance of the invaders. Both South Korean and U.S. forces took a last stand in the Pusan region in the southeastern corner of the peninsula east of the Naktong River.

Realizing the grave danger to the existence of the Republic of Korea, President Truman requested the assistance of U.N. members for South Korea. The Security Council of the U.N. condemned North Korea as an aggressor and asked the member nations to provide military and other assistance to South Korea. The United States and 15 other nations joined the war to repel the aggressors and the United Nations forces were organized.

An American general, Douglas MacArthur, Supreme Commander of the Allied Forces in the Pacific (SCAP), was named Commander of the U.N. forces in Korea. Meanwhile, the U.S. Army, Navy, Air Force and Marines arrived in Korea, and with the arrival of other U.N. troops from Great Britain, France, Canada, Australia and other countries, a counterattack was launched. The surprise landing of the U.N. forces at Inch'ŏn on September 15 isolated North Korean troops in the south, and they were destroyed.

On September 28, Seoul was recovered, and under the authorization given by the U.N. and the U.S. government, U.S. and South Korean troops crossed the 38th parallel in pursuit of the fleeing North Korean troops. On October 19, the U.N. forces captured the North Korean capital of P'yŏngyang, and the U.N. forces reached the Yalu River on the western front and Ch'ŏngjin on the eastern front.

The collapse of Communist North Korea was imminent, but in the middle of October over 150,000 Chinese Communist troops poured into Korea from Manchuria and an "entirely new war" in Korea began.

Opposite page: U.N. troops retook Seoul and raised Korean flag.

A South Korean war orphan and the scene of destruction.

The truce was signed, but no peace was established.

The U.N. forces withdrew from North Korea during the winter of 1950, and the Chinese and North Korean forces pushed southward across the 38th parallel, Seoul again being captured by the aggressors on January 4, 1951. However, the counterattack of the U.N. forces in March pushed back the aggressors beyond the 38th parallel, and a stalemate developed. The tide of the war gradually turned against North Korea.

The North Koreans proposed a truce through the Soviet Union, and talks began between the representatives of the two sides in the summer of 1951. But the truce talk progressed slowly. With the death of Joseph Stalin in early 1953 the North Koreans were anxious to end the war. As a result, the Korean Armistice was signed on July 27,

1953, and the four mile-wide demilitarized zone (DMZ) was established across the peninsula along the battle fronts. With this, the truce village of P'anmunjŏm was put on the Korean map.

The North Korean ambition to conquer South Korea by force failed, but the war caused enormously heavy property damage in South Korea and no less than 2 million war casualties. Some two million North Koreans escaped to South Korea, fleeing from the Communists.

In 1954, a mutual security treaty between the United States and South Korea was concluded, and with this, U.S. military aid to the Republic began in order to strengthen the country's armed forces. However, the Geneva Conference which was held in that year failed to establish peace in Korea. The war which the north Korean Communists started only made the people in South Korea more anti-Communism.

THE FIRST REPUBLIC

During the Korean War, President Rhee, supported by his Liberal Party, became increasingly oppressive and autocratic, and changes in the constitution were made for their own benefit. The constitutional amendments made in 1952 and 1954 and the suppression of the opposition Democratic Party created strong resentment particularly on the part of intellectuals and students. The Liberal Party-sponsored constitutional amendment in 1954 gave President Rhee lifetime tenure in office.

The division of Korea imposed a restraint on the economy of South Korea which had been primarily an agricultural zone with some industries, mostly light industries. Its area was smaller (37,060 sq. miles, or 98,555 sq. km) than that of the north (48,240 sq. miles, or 122,370 sq. km.). The entire area of

Hqs. of the Liberal Party in Seoul.

South Korea was 45% of the peninsula, but it had more than 2/3 of the population.

Although the First Republic was able to maintain national security and bring about educational progress, it failed to improve economic conditions of the people. Unemployment was high, and the shortage of food, fuel, clothing, and housing was critical. Only relief goods provided by the United Nations and the United States prevented mass starvation.

THE APRIL STUDENT UPRISING

The popular resentment against the government and the Liberal Party which had been growing exploded in 1960. The corruptive means with which the Liberal Party conducted

109

THE MAY MILITARY REVOLUTION AND THE THIRD AND FOURTH REPUBLICS

The new bicameral legislative body of the National Assembly amended the constitution, and elected Yun Po-sŏn president. President Yun appointed Chang Myŏn (John Chang) premier. With this the Second Republic emerged in July 1960. The new government and the ruling Democratic Party were unable to improve economic conditions, show their political leadership, or control the growing Communist influence in South Korea. Threats from the north increased as the state of confusion grew worse.

Mindful of the increasing threats to the nation from the north, General Pak Chung-hee and other young Army officers carried out the military revolution of May 16, 1961. The revolutionaries quickly put Seoul under military occupation and established a junta.

Social stability was restored, and political parties — the Democratic Republican and the New Democratic — reappeared. The First Five-Year Economic Development Plan was put into effect in 1962. In accordance with the pledge made by the junta in May 1961, a new constitution was adopted, elections were carried out in October 1963, and General Pak, the presidential candidate of the Democratic Republican Party who retired from the military was elected president by a large majority of popular vote. Elections held in November elected the new unicameral National Assembly with the Democratic Republican Party as majority.

On December 17, 1963, the Third Republic emerged. It successfully concluded its First Five-Year Economic Development Plan in 1966. President Pak was re-elected in 1967 and in that year the Second Five-Year Economic Development Plan began.

In the early 1970s, there was a dramatic

The Army joined students against the government of President Rhee.

politics and manipulated elections in the March 15, 1960 elections for president and vice-president demonstrations on the part of students. They demanded that the election results of the March 15 elections declared null and void.

On April 19, 1960 tens of thousands students in Seoul, joined by professors and citizenry, carried out a mass demonstration. They marched toward the presidential mansion as they demanded the resignation of President Rhee and the vice-president. Troops were mobilized when the police were unable to control the demonstrators, but the troops refused to act against the students.

Thus, President Rhee and his cabinet resigned and the First Republic ended in April 1960. The April 19 student uprising is regarded as the first people's rights movement in Korean history and the one which demonstrated the democratic potentials of the Korean people.

Gen. Pak who led the May 16 Military Revolution, directs his men.

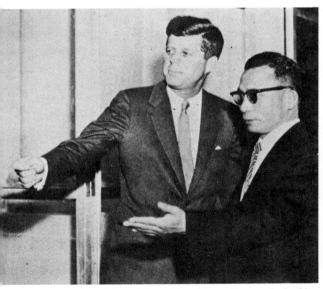

Gen. Pak paid a visit to President Kennedy in November, 1961 and received U.S. support.

change in the international economic situation, particularly in the Far East. The situation in Vietnam worsened, and the oil shock had enormous negative impact on the Korean

The Seoul-Pusan super highway.

A night view of P'ohang Iron and Steel Co., which has an expanded annual capacity of 2,000,000 tons.

economy as well. President Richard Nixon's China visit in 1972 altered the international situation in East Asia radically.

The new constitution, called *yusin*, of the Fourth Republic, which gave extraordinary power to the president to enact emergency measures, further limited freedom of speech and press. The government became increasingly autocratic, infringing upon human rights in a variety of ways and the absence of the freedom of speech and press was conspicuous.

The Fourth Republic successfully carried out the Fourth and the Fifth Five-Year Economic Development plans, and brought about a rapid economic growth, bringing the Korean economy to what Professor W. W. Rostow called "the take-off stage."

However, following the re-election of President Pak in July 1978 and the December elections for new members of the National Assembly, anti-government agitation by students supported by the opposition party increased. The students demanded the abolition of the *yusin* constitution. The growing anti-government student demonstrations created serious political percussion. At the same time, President Jimmy Carter's threat to withdraw all U. S. ground troops from South Korea

only made the political situation in the country more tense and dangerous.

At this critical juncture, President Pak was assassinated by Kim Chae-gyu, Director of the Korean CIA, on October 26, 1979. With the death of President Pak, the Fourth Republic collapsed and Premier Ch'oe Kyu-ha became president of the interregnum government.

The Third and the Fourth Republic of Korea under President Pak achieved much, especially in economic development. The First Five-Year Economic Development Plan which began in 1962 laid the foundation for industrialization of the economy, paying particular attention to the development of natural resources. The Second Five-Year Economic Development Plan that began in 1967 concentrated on the elevation of the level of electronic, chemical, steel and machine industries. The Third Five-Year Plan of 1972 and 1976 was concentrated in developing manufacturing and heavy industry. The Fourth Five-Year Economic Development Plan that began in 1977 and ended in 1981 brought about further economic growth and modernization of the Korean economy.

These five-year economic development plans achieved an average annual rate of

The New Community Movement and the mechanization of farming.

GNP growth of 10.2% between 1961 and 1976, as the dollar value increased from $2,124 million in 1961 to $25,090 in 1976 and $30,676 in 1980. Per capita GNP grew from $86 in 1962 to $1,500 in 1980. The amount of food grains produced grew from 5.5 million metric tons in 1961 to 9.0 million metric tons in 1978. Meanwhile, Korea's export increased from $40 million in 1961 to $20,000 million in 1981. The Korean economy grew to such a point that by 1976 U. S. economic aid was no longer needed.

Meanwhile, some 156,000 Korean workers went abroad in the 1970s, and the Korean construction firms in foreign countries made a great contribution to the economic development at home with their earnings. Some 115,000 Korean workers who went to the Middle East alone earned and brought back home some $5,700 million.

The New Community Movement was launched in 1971 to improve economic conditions of rural Korea as well as to achieve a

The new farm village.

113

The National Museum in Kyŏngbok palace.

The National Assembly building.

The National Assembly of Korea.

balanced development of agriculture and industry. It was also aimed at the promotion of agricultural modernization—mechanization, scientific farming—as well as the elevation of cultural and social standards of the rural population. It also endeavored to promote national consciousness and the spirit of mutual cooperation among the people. The model of the New Community Movement has been exported to many developing nations of Africa, Asia and Latin America.

With the rise of an educated population, the cultural level of the Koreans was elevated. While promoting the revival movement for traditional culture, the Koreans brought about the development of modern culture in a variety of ways. As a result, the number of public and private museums and libraries, cultural societies, centers for performing arts, and theaters grew immensely. Despite the limited freedom of press, six major daily newspapers and local papers contributed much to the dissemination of information. Korea also became one of the nations in the world which produced the most books, monthlies, and weeklies per capita.

THE FIFTH REPUBLIC

After the death of President Pak, the nation faced a serious social disorder. At this conjuncture the government proclaimed martial law to restore law and order. Then Martial Law Command, General Chun Doohwan took over the government suspended the 1972 constitution, dissolved the National Assembly, banned all political activities. Under the new constitution General Chun, who had retired from the military, was elected the president of the Fifth Republic. In his inaugural address, on March 3, 1981, President Chun pledged to build a "democratic welfare society" of Korea.

114

8 *KOREA TODAY*

Strong national defense forces.

Korea is no longer the underdeveloped nation that she was in 1945. She is a thriving and progressive nation proud of what she has accomplished since her liberation. Her communication and transportation systems are modern, her educational and cultural standards are high, and her economy and military are strong. Korea's population today is 38.5 million.

The Republic of Korea has a republican form of government with a strong presidency, and its government, political parties and people are endeavoring to promote a democratic way of life. The people are sophisticated and eager to exercise their rights. Korea's natural resources are scarce, she does not produce oil, and she imports a tremendous amount of raw materials. However, the country is almost self-sufficient in terms of food production, and displays all the potential of bringing about even greater economic progress.

After suffering a serious economic recession in 1980, Korea made a rapid economic recovery and achieved a GNP growth of 5.6 per cent in 1981. Korea's GNP in 1981 was $57,600 million with a per capita GNP of $1,500, and she exported about $20,000 million worth of manufactured goods. The Koreans are confident of achieving the goals of the Fifth Five-Year Economic Development Plan which began in 1982.

Religious freedom is staunchly maintained in the Republic. The dominant religion is

Buddhism, but the influence of Christianity is strong. Shamanism is still practiced by a minority, and Islam which has recently been introduced to Korea has won many converts.

Koreans are achievement oriented and are willing to make sacrifices to educate their children. Although Korea is a small country, there are over 6 million pupils in six-year primary schools under a compulsory education law. There are over 3 million in the three-year middle schools, and 1.5 million are in the three-year high schools. Another 650,000 students are attending secondary level vocational and technical schools, and some 500,000 are attending colleges and universities. The rate of illiteracy (0.5%) is among the lowest in the world.

Opposite page: (Above) Korean workers in the Middle Eastern country.
(Below) Korean-made cars exported to all corners of the world.

A Korean university and students.

The Buddhists on Buddha's birthday.

Myongdong Cathedral in Seoul.

The Korean soccer team playing the game.

At present, the entire population of the Republic is involved in the New Community Movement that began in 1971. Although it was inaugurated to modernize rural areas and increase farm income, it became a national movement involving all segments of the population. Its basic aims are to promote the virtues of diligence, self-help and co-operation.

With the growing economy and education, the Republic of Korea is a country which is strong in sports. Korea's athletes are competing in the international arena, and her table tennis, volley ball, basket ball, soccer and boxing teams have made enviable records by winning games in international meets all over the world. Korea hosted numerous international sports events in the 1970s, and she is designated as the host nation for the 1986 Asian Olympics and the 1988 Olympic games.

Taegwŏndo, a Korea-originated martial art, is spreading fast both in Korea and abroad.

The Republic of Korea maintains friendly relations with some 103 nations, and the number of the Third World countries which establish diplomatic relations with Korea is growing. Korea's wish to join the United Nations has not been granted, but her representatives at the United Nations as observers have gained the respect of member nations.

The visit of the United States by President Chun Doo-hwan in early 1981 and his cordial talks with President Ronald Reagan resulted in improved relations between the two countries. This, together with increased close relations with Southeast Asian countries where President Chun toured in the summer of 1981, improved Korea's international image considerably. Meanwhile, Korea seeks

Right: President Chun Doo-hwan greets with the Korean resident in the U.S.

Below: International conference held in Seoul.

to expand her relations with non-hostile Communist nations.

All efforts made by the government of the Republic of Korea since August 15, 1970, failed to open dialogue between the two states, although on July 4, 1972, the two Korean governments issued a joint statement to open talks to settle the Korean question by peaceful means without outside intervention. However, the political dialogue which began in the fall of 1972 was unilaterally suspended by North Korea in 1973. North Korea even refused to cooperate with the South Korean Red Cross in an attempt to unify scattered families in both areas.

The north Korean Communists refused to accept the proposal made by the late President Pak in July 1979 to re-open the talks, as well as President Chun's proposal of January 1982. While insisting on South Korea's acceptance of their own unworkable plans for the unification of Korea, the north Korean Communists constantly agitate for the withdrawal of all U.S. troops and the overthrow of the government of the Republic.

Be that it may, with the rapidly developing culture and society and ever-growing economic strength, the Republic of Korea looks forward with confidence to achieving the historic mission of the people to unify their divided country and establish a modern democratic welfare society in Korea.

The Unification Road between Seoul and P'an-munjŏm.

EPILOGUE

Throughout her long history, because of her geographical location, Korea has encountered cultural influence from abroad as well as external threats to her very existence. However, as we have seen in the preceding chapters, the Koreans have succeeded in surmounting various hardships.

The Koreans are the people who admire chrysanthemums blooming in the frost, plum blossoms in the snow, bamboo in the wind and lotus blooming from the muddy lake bottom. With such sentiments and resilient racial characteristics, they have preserved their ancient heritage. Synthesizing their own culture with that of others, they have created a culture uniquely their own. In the recent past, the Korean people brought about a remarkable economic development which they proudly call "the miracle on the Han River," transforming an agricultural nation into a modern, industrial society.

Rabindranath Tagore (1861–1941), an eminent Indian philosopher, once said about Korea:

Korea, once a bright light
Of the Golden Age of Asia.
If it is relit, it will be
The light of the East.

The Republic of Korea, with its astonishing success in economic development and industrialization, rapid educational and cultural growth, and its creative psychological and social reconstruction programs of the New Community Movement, has indeed became a bright light in the Far East.

INDEX

Haein, temple of, 30
Hamel, Hendrik, 62
Han China, 15
Han River, 17, 18
Handicraft, 34
Han'gŭl, 55, 78, 88
History of Ancient Korea, 63
Hodge, John R., 100
Hŏryū temple, 27
Hunmin chŏngŭm, see *Han'gul*
Hwang Chin-i, 56
Hwangsŏng sinmun, 93
Hwanung, the myth of, 14
Hwarang, 19
Hwarangdo, 19, 21
Hwimun school, 73
hyangak (native music), 46
hyangga (native songs), 37
Hyech'o, Monk, 30
Hyeja, Monk, 27

Idu, the system of, 22
Inch'ŏn, 73, 77, during the Korean War, 106
Independence, Declaration of, 95
Independence, Korean, 100; U. S. policy, 100
Independence Arch, 87
Independence Club, 87, 88
The Independent (newspaper), 87, 88
India, Korean monk in, 30
Industrial development, Japanese period, 94
Iron culture, 15
Iron, produced in Korea, 15
Iron weapons, production of, 16
Isolation, policy of, 73
Itō Hirobumi, death of, 93

Jaisohn, Philip, see Sŏ Chae-p'il
Japan, relation with the Yi dynasty, 73–74; war with China, 83
Japanese annexation of Korea, 90–93
Japanese emperor, Imperial Rescript of, 94
Japanese Imperial Army, mobilization of Koreans into, 99
Japanese invasions of, 18, 59; effects of, 61, 62, 76
Japanese pirates, 49
Japanese policy in Korea, 1910–45, 94, 97, 98, 99
Japanese protectorate over Korea, 91
Jurched, invasion of, 40; effects of, 47

Kang Kam-ch'an, 40
Kanghwa Island, 42, 73–76

Kanghwa Treaty, 76
Kangsŏ, Koguryŏ tombs in, 23
Kapo Reform, 85
Kapsin chŏngbyŏn (coup d'etat of 1884), 79, 80
Kaya, States of, 11; the Japanese invasion, 18; Silla invasion and the fall of, 17
Kayagŭm (musical instrument of Kaya), 46
Khitan, invasion of, 40; effects of, 42
Kim Chae-gyu, 112
Kim Chŏng-ho, 63
Kim Chong-hŭi (Ch'usa/Wandang), 70
Kim Chwa-jin, General, 98
Kim clan, of Silla, 29
Kim Hong-do (Tanwŏn), 64
Kim Il-sung, 102, 103
Kim Ku, 98
Kim Ok-kyun, 80
Kim Pu-sik, 44
Kim Tae-gŏn, 72
Kim Tŭk-sin, 64
kisaeng (female entertainers), 68
Koguryŏ, alliance with Paekche, 17; The aristocracy of, 18; Buddhism in, 20; cultural contribution to Japan, 26; fall of, 28; political evolution in, 17; the rise of, 14; the territorial expansion of, 16; wars with Paekche, 17; wars with Sui China, 18; wars with T'ang China, 18
Kojong, King (emperor after 1897), 72, 78, 79; flight to Russian Legation, 85, 86; abdication of 93
Kŏmundo, British occupation of, 80
kŏmun'go (musical instrument of Koguryŏ), 22, 46
Korea, coast lines of, 10; mountain ranges, 10; rivers of, 12; seasons of, 10; size of, 10
Korea, Republic of, April student uprising, 109, 110; Chinese troops in, 106; Communists in, 104; cultural development, 114; economic development, 112, 115; economic development plans, 110–113; educational development, 109; effects of the war, 109; end of the Fourth Republic, 112; establishment of, 103; fall of the First Republic, 109; Fifth Republic, 114; First Republic, 104–109; military revolution in, 110; new Assembly, 110; New Community Movement

in, 113,114; North Korean invasion of, 104–105; Second Republic, 110; Third and Fourth Republic, 110–114; U. N. troops in, 106; U. S. Korea relations, 110
Korean armistice, 108
Korean Army, dissolution of, 91; Republic of Korea, 104
Korean Army for National Restoration, in China, 97; in Manchuria, 98
Korean communists, in South Korea, 103; North Korean, 104, 120
Korean Declaration of Independence, 95
Korean mission to Japan, 77, 78
Korean mission to Russia, 85, 86
Korean mission to the United States, 77, 78
Korean War, 104–109; armistice, 108; effects of, 108, 109
Koryŏsa (History of Koryŏ), 63
Koryŏ, the absorption of Silla, 35; art of, 45; architecture of, 45; Buddhism in, 43; celadons of, 47, 68; coinage of, 40; Confucian influence in, 42; culture of, 45; defense structure of, 43; districts of, 38; economy of, 40; fall of, 49; festivals of, 40; foreign trade of, 40; the founding of, 38; grain system of, 39, 40; gun powder production in, 45; Japanese pirates, 49; military affairs, 42; the Mongols invasions of, 45, music of, 46 poetry of, 47; printing in, 43; religion of, 30, 43; social system of, 39; songs of, 46; wars with the Khitan and the Jurched, 42
Kudaragi, tree of Paekche in Japan, 27
Kŭmgang Mount, painting of, 64
Kŭmgwan, tomb of, 24
Kungnaesong (former capital of Koguryŏ), 16
Kŭnch'ogo, King, 17
Kwanggaet'o, King, 16
Kwiju, battle of, 40
Kyŏngbok Palace, reconstruction of, 74
Kyŏngch'on temple, 45
Kyŏnghoeru pavilion, 58
Kyŏngju, capital of Silla, 18, 23, 34

Lacquer ware manufacturing in Silla, 29
Landlordism, 55
Lantern festival of Koryŏ, 40